Is This a Funny Story?

Is This a Funny Story?

A Stage-Four Memoir

ELLEN VANSTONE

sh.
SUTHERLAND HOUSE

TORONTO, 2026

Sutherland House
416 Moore Ave., Suite 304
Toronto, ON M4G 1C9

First edition, September 2026

If you are interested in inviting one of our authors to a live event or media appearance, please contact sranasinghe@sutherlandhousebooks.com and visit our website at sutherlandhousebooks.com for more information.

We acknowledge the support of the Government of Canada.

Manufactured in Canada
Cover designed by Jason Logan and Jordan Lunn
Book composed by Karl Hunt

Library and Archives Canada Cataloguing in Publication
Title: Is this a funny story? : a stage-four memoir / Ellen Vanstone.
Names: Vanstone, Ellen, author
Description: First edition.
Identifiers: Canadiana (print) 20260174882 | Canadiana (ebook) 20260174890 | ISBN 9781997701590 (softcover) | ISBN 9781997701705 (EPUB)
Subjects: LCSH: Vanstone, Ellen. | LCSH: Melanoma—Patients—Canada—Biography. | LCGFT: Autobiographies.
Classification: LCC RC280.M37 V36 2026 | DDC 616.99/4770092—dc23

ISBN 978-1-997701-59-0
eBook ISBN 978-1-997701-70-5

For Eliza

Contents

2022

1

“Cancer”

I’m sitting in my car in an empty, unlit parking lot outside a decrepit warehouse between the railroad tracks and the Red River. It’s peaceful. You’d never know you were in the city, let alone a stone’s throw from its most notorious intersection, a tangled mess of merging arteries, randomly placed traffic lights, nonsensical turning lanes, and angry drivers. Locals call it Confusion Corner. It’s been memorialized as a vector of despair in a song by the Weakerthans, a band known for such catchy lyrics as “I hate Winnipeg!”

But here, inside my little car, hidden by the raised embankment of the tracks, the hum of the engine muffled by layers of falling snow, I don’t hear a thing. I’ve just picked up my labradoodle Sally from the doggy daycare in the warehouse, and I’m considering my return journey across the gaping potholes and jagged ice shelves of the abandoned field that passes for the warehouse's parking lot. So I sit and watch the gently falling snow, which at least makes the terrain look smoother and more navigable.

I think about sitting in the car like this with my daughter when she was little. We'd arrive home from her school or music lesson or playdate, and then, after I turned off the car, neither of us would move. We'd sit in silent harmony or talk about nothing, until one of us started to get cold, and then we'd sigh and unbuckle and head indoors.

But on this night, my daughter is grown, living in our condo in Toronto, while I sit out the pandemic in my hometown. I'm living in a broken-down bungalow in my old neighborhood, indulging in an extended experiment of "can you go home again?" If the answer turns out to be yes, I'll sell the Toronto condo, replace my rotting shack with a cute, new, architect-designed bungalow, and retire here in relative luxury. After two years, I still haven't decided.

My phone rings.

"My name's Nicole," says a youngish-sounding woman. "I'm a nurse navigator at Cancer Care Manitoba."

My first impulse is to say: Cancer Care Manitoba? Well, bully for you, Nicole. I'm sure your parents must be very proud. But what's it got to do with *me*?

Instead, I say, "Oh."

Nicole explains that Cancer Care Manitoba is reviewing the results of my recent biopsy, which should take about a week, and then she'll get back to me.

I'm confused. How does Cancer Care Manitoba even know I had a biopsy? I don't have a family doctor. After I noticed a lump at the top of my left leg a couple of months ago, I went to a walk-in clinic on Corydon Avenue, which led to a series of doctors sending me for a series of tests, culminating in a biopsy of my left inguinal lymph node at St. Boniface Hospital a week ago.

The doctor and technician are nice—everyone is nice in Winnipeg—but the procedure is unpleasant. They have me lie on a gurney with my leg and groin on display while they use ultrasound to line up the lump on screen so the doctor knows exactly where to aim his giant needle. Then, a jab and *kerchunk!* as he pulls the trigger to extract the core sample.

I watch the first two extractions, then close my eyes and think of other things, like how my car is illegally parked outside the front entrance. It's a bitterly cold day, and when my Winnipeg parking app didn't work, I got out of the car and tried my Visa card in the machine. After three futile attempts to make it work, my frozen fingers fumbled the card into the gutter between the waist-high snowbank and my car. Worried about being late for the biopsy, I left it there. If anyone wanted to shovel out a four-foot-high snowbank to steal my credit card, they were welcome to it.

Now, lying on the gurney, trying not to think about the groin-drilling excavation, I worry about getting a parking ticket. It's a primo spot right outside the main entrance—would that make the ticket more expensive? How much was a parking ticket in Winnipeg these days? Fifty dollars? Sixty? I could afford that. So why am I suddenly so agitated about getting a ticket? Also, aren't people with cancer supposed to be ultra-chill about mundane matters like parking tickets? Why aren't I chill about this? *Ah*, I thought, *it's because, technically speaking, I don't have cancer*. At least not yet. The biopsy jury is still out. In fact, worrying about a parking ticket is a reasonable and normal thing to do while lying on a gurney getting drilled with a giant needle.

When they're finally done, I quickly dress and race out to my car. No ticket! This is a good sign. It's lucky. I'm a lucky person, privileged, with no real worries in the world at all. I drive home and forget all about it.

Except now this Nicole person is calling, and she's saying the word "cancer." But it doesn't really count because she has no actual news. Results are pending. She'll call back in a week. I put it back out of my mind. Even if I wanted to worry, I don't have time. My life is full of family, and dog walking, and shoveling my car out of snowbanks, and work.

2
Diggstown

My work is writing and story-editing scripts for TV drama. Right now, I'm working full-time in a writers' room for a CBC drama series called *Diggstown*. It's about a cool, successful Legal Aid lawyer in Halifax who fights for a different down-and-out client each week, while dealing with a crisis in her own past, which we, the writers, will force her to confront and resolve before she can win cases and find true love.

I join a Zoom meeting of about eight to ten people every day to break episodes, which means coming up with sixty or so scenes per show on a digital storyboard. Once our showrunner Floyd is satisfied we have a viable episode, one of the writers will go off with the scene-by-scene digital road map to cobble together a first draft.

In all my years of working on various TV shows, *Diggstown* is the best experience by far, albeit with one downside. As an elderly white lady in a room full of young people of color, I am reminded every single day of how unwoke and unconsciously racist I am in the assumptions I make about Marcie Diggs, the Black main character. About her choices, or her jeopardy in various situations, on the street, at a country club, or in the courtroom. I cringe at all the dumb shit I've said, and thank the lord that my young colleagues are so patient with me.

On the other hand, I do have my uses. I am preternaturally good at writing dialogue for elderly, evil white characters, like the residential school nun lying through her Catholic-church-aided-and-abetted teeth about her abuse of a plaintiff back in the day, her flinty eyes boring into him across the courtroom with such malign intensity, he has a panic attack and flees, jeopardizing the whole case. Or the way I effortlessly inhabit the skin of an old, rich white guy who uses his patriarchal entitlement and influence to entrap Marcie in a stock-raiding scheme that puts her under his thumb for the entire next season. Or my deft depiction of the manipulative, wealthy publisher matriarch who tries to frame a Black kid for a murder her own spoiled-brat son committed.

What I've never been able to write properly is dialogue for Marcie. I don't understand her. I keep trying to write her scenes as if I were her, injecting my own brand of (oh God, kill me now) jaunty boomer archness to her dialogue. Which my boss Floyd duly removes in his showrunner passes on the shooting scripts. In frustration, one day I finally tell him I don't get Marcie and could he please explain her to me.

"Marcie is me," shrugs Floyd, as if stating the obvious. "She's angry—*all the time*." Note that Floyd is one of the most congenial, kind, and cheerful people I've ever met. So I learn something about him in this moment. I can't pretend to relate to his experience as a Black man in contemporary society. But I can strongly relate to female anger in any form. So while I'll never get Marcie Diggs right in my scripts, I feel a bit closer to what motivates her.

Besides my day job on *Diggstown*, I've been doing what all TV writers are constantly doing, which is developing other shows. Producers pay you anywhere from nothing to a few thousand bucks to come up with a main character, a premise, a pilot episode, season arc, and series arc, which you then pitch to the networks in hopes of getting a series order. Sometimes the idea originates with the writer. Other times, it's an adaptation of a book or someone else's idea. The development phase can take years, and the money's terrible, but the dream of getting your own show, making one that's actually good, and making lots of money is irresistible.

One of the shows I'm developing is an adaptation of a book in which a retired male cop retires to a small town where an Indigenous female teen has been gang-raped and murdered—*Record scratch! No, no, no!*

Ah, people, when I'm in charge of the world, no show will ever again start with a fuckable female's dead body. No dead bodies whatsoever will be lovingly displayed in a morgue where everyone, from director to crew to, later, viewers at home, will be jerked out of the story and forced to ponder the "dead" woman's fully alive tits or body type or bikini wax.

Nor shall there be a beleaguered, shambolic, "misunderstood" man-boy detective who's actually a deeply conventional patriarchal archetype laboring under the disapproval of a stern ex-wife who's too cunty to put up with his rugged-individualist way of whoring/gambling/drinking/being emotionally shut off. Nor will any male hero in my TV universe have the attendant trope of a sexy daughter who gives her daddy lots of guff, but loves him unconditionally—unlike her mother, the cunty ex-wife. Why do so many shows—from *Castle* and *Wallender* to *Bosch*, *Landman*, *The Agency*, *Shetland*—feature men with infinitely forgiving, fuckable daughters? Why aren't there more shows, like *Lupin* and *Hijack*, that feature flawed dads trying to become the role models their beloved sons need?

Meanwhile, since I'm not in charge of the world, I do what I can to change things. In the show about the retired male cop, I've replaced the violently murdered Indigenous girl in the tease with a dead, blond, white boy, and made the main character a middle-aged lady cop going through a messy divorce, who's forced to face her demons before she can win cases and find true love.

On another project, a young woman inadvertently kills her faithless fiancé on the first night in their luxury New York Style co-op apartment, then covers up the death so she can keep the lease, but is forced to face her demons before she can find true love. On another project, a young woman marries a rich Australian iron ore miner, only to discover he's a 300-year-old organ-harvested monster cultivating his offspring, so she has to team up with his pregnant mistresses to kill him and save the babies—all while facing her own personal demons before she can find true love.

And so on, with various other pitches for producers in Toronto and the UK. The time difference means I can work full-time on *Diggstown* during the day, and deal with overseas calls during the night and early morning.

It's pleasant work. I sit in my little bungalow office in Winnipeg, squinting into the low winter sun that travels across the bare branches of the trees in the park across the street each day, marveling that I'm being paid to make up stories and hang out with lovely young writers half my age who kindly keep me on my toes.

As for Nicole, it's been more than a week since she was supposed to call me back—three weeks, in fact—but I haven't given it any thought.

Then, on March 14, 2022, at 10:15 a.m. Central Standard Time (I take thorough notes), the phone rings.

Luckily it's during the fifteen-minute morning pee-and-tea break from the *Diggstown* room—just enough time to put on the kettle and triple-check that my Zoom screen is muted while I quickly go to the bathroom, because my bungalow is very small and the sliding door to the bathroom is stuck in the open position. Then I make my tea and eat a snack before we're all back on camera. The snack is important. Pre-Covid, when writers met in person, a writers' room would be filled with beverages, a coffee machine, fresh fruit that one would virtuously eat in the mornings, and chips, chocolate, and junk food that were impossible to resist in the afternoon. It was easy to eat and drink discreetly, because you could scarf it all down whenever all heads turned to whoever was talking at any given moment.

Now, disastrously, in a Zoom room, your face is on camera the whole time. It's disgusting to watch people chew onscreen. Thus, snacking during breaks is a key priority. I tell Nicole I only have a minute.

She gets straight to the point.

"The test results from your biopsy came back. They're positive for malignancy."

Only once before in my life has a telephone call made my legs go weak and forced me to sit down. That was thirty years earlier, when a fertility clinic nurse called me to say the IVF had worked and I was pregnant. Except this time, there isn't a darling baby gestating in my womb, but a toxic mass brewing in my groin.

I pick up a pen. "So it's lymphoma? Like, hopefully, the good kind?"

Nicole hesitates. She sounds kind of . . . rattled?

"No," she says. "The reason the biopsy results took so long is that they were so . . . unexpected. It had to go back to the team for more discussion." She pauses. I wait. "It's metastatic melanoma."

I don't know what that means. Lymphoma. Melanoma. Tomato, tuh-mah-toh?

She keeps talking while I try to keep up with my notes: Inguinal lymph node measures 3 cm; multiple pulmonary nodules; liver has a 1.4 cm spot; there's a tumor beside the vaginal vault; no aggressive bone lesions; an uncertain 1.2 cm nodule in the hysterectomy bed; upcoming appointments with a surgeon, or medical oncologist; CT scan; triaging by the Skin Group; testing for a BRAF gene mutation . . .

The call ends just in time for me to rejoin the Zoom room, where I'm totally fine. If anything, I'm hyper-focused on the story problems at hand. Like, should Marcie Diggs's ex-boyfriend Avery testify against her when she's investigated on trumped-up charges of misbehavior in court? Or will he stay true to Marcie and say "the results are inconclusive" to get her off the hook?

The only difference is a disturbance in my eyesight. It's as if there's a rolling news feed at the bottom of my field of vision, like the headlines you see running along the bottom of round-the-clock local news channel CP24. Except my headlines aren't about a car crash or house fire. It's just one simple phrase, scrolling over and over: *You have cancer. You have cancer. You have cancer . . .*

3

Taking Notes

I spend March and April in Winnipeg worrying about money. Not knowing what's in store for me in terms of time and treatment, I've told my agent to get me out of all my deals, instructing him to tell clients I'm on a full-time project elsewhere. Technically true. But without work, I can no longer afford to sit in my prairie bungalow mulling over whether to retire in my hometown of Winnipeg, surrounded by family or in Toronto surrounded by friends.

The family is two elder sisters and three younger brothers, who come with all the attendant annoyances of any set of siblings. But they are also loyal and helpful, always ready to take me shopping for food, hardware supplies, or a giant, down-filled jacket for winter. Or my brother M.K.V. shows up out of the blue to fix the broken railings on my front steps, but doesn't bother knocking to say hello before, during, or after. Or

Jay shows up with a computer cord I didn't know I needed. Or Linday secretly takes out all my garbage and recycling, making sure I don't know it's him or what he's doing. It's like we're all in some kind of stoicism contest, though I'm not sure what the prize is. I, meanwhile, have become the obnoxious Toronto person who believes in social niceties and open declarations of emotion and hugging, which makes me the annoying one as I try to make them change, you know, *for their own good!*

So if I stay in Winnipeg, I know I'll have family support, day or night. But then I factor in that Princess Margaret Cancer Centre in Toronto is one of the best cancer hospitals in the world. Except—and this is a sign of my deteriorating mental state—what if I tell my Winnipeg oncology team that I want to be treated in Toronto? And then if I don't end up going to Toronto, what if they hold a grudge against me and, instead of trying to cure me, they try to kill me? I dither and go to various medical appointments at Cancer Care Manitoba—bloodwork, ultrasound, X-rays, bone scan, PET scans, CT scans, MRIs, questionnaires, ECGs. Finally, in May, I work up the courage to tell my oncology doctor at Cancer Care Manitoba that I must return to Toronto "for financial reasons." She practically whoops with delight. "I can get you an appointment at Princess Margaret next week," she says. "I'll make the call today."

I pack up my bungalow as much as I can, call a number on a flyer to sell it privately to a house flipper, and leave the rest to my siblings. My brother L.P. books off work so he can drive Sally and me to Toronto to get to my first appointment in time. His world-class stoicism means our conversation is firmly based on "need to know" rather than the blathering gossip and unfiltered yakking I prefer.

And so, six days after leaving Winnipeg, I attend my first appointment with my oncologist, a dramatic Italian lady who flies to her home in Lake Como on a regular basis to get her hair done. She terrifies me. My M.O. with health-care providers at this stage is a combination of violent sucking up and hysteria-tinged joke-making to show that *I'm really no trouble at all, I don't even take my own illness seriously, you don't need to worry about me being a burden!* My humor is at the level of dad jokes—indeed, I literally repeat my dad's old jokes. For example, when the doctor says, "immunotherapy involves a combination of the drugs ipilimumab and nivolumab," I laugh and quip, "Easy for you to say!" She stares back at me with a mixture of confusion and bloodcurdling Italian disdain, then proceeds as if I have not spoken.

I'm sorry to report that this only makes me try harder. For months, at every appointment, I'm like a jerky puppet, jumping around verbally, trying to impress, trying to take control of the conversation—only to feel more and more out of control. My routine turns into several trips a week, going to Princess Margaret to repeat all the tests that were done in Winnipeg, with a few more thrown in. As I understand it, they need to know exactly what kind of cancer I have, and where in my body it might have spread to, before they decide on a course of treatment.

On each visit, I stride into the main lobby and see cancer patients in wheelchairs, or limping on one leg after a presumed amputation, clutching onto companions for support, coughing, groaning, looking ill. Even the little security guard who shuffles by, frail and wheezing, looks like he's done for. The second I start dodging my way through the *Walking Dead* phalanx of cancer victims, my posture snaps straighter, and I stride with strength and purpose. Make no mistake, people. I am not one of you. I am here temporarily, in error. An error which shall be rectified through the sheer force of my will, as I bend everyone to my point of view with my plucky spirit and banter.

As mentioned, I take thorough notes. All writers take notes. My home is littered with scraps of paper and scribblers filled with story ideas, some questionable (*Dog needs new kidney—she kidnaps another dog*), some good (*Mrs. Hudson, the real brains behind Sherlock and Watson—she & Irene Adler secretly solve Sherlock's cases over coffee in Baker Street kitchen*). Other notes address relationships and family issues, none of which shall ever see the light of day.

For my trips to Princess Margaret, I buy a brand-new scribbler and diligently make entries before, during, and after appointments. I record details about the people around me, or about the food, or about the building, like the number of steps between each level of the lobby stairwell that runs from the basement to the fifth floor (*twenty-five steps, twenty steps, twenty-eight steps, twenty-five—why would the architects make it inconsistent? They must have a reason*).

During appointments, I write down everything without understanding most of it: BRAF mutation = atypical requires further molecular testing; liver lesions in segment seven, difficulty in imaging; multiple pulmonary nodules; chemotherapy is not immunotherapy = systemic approach.

At one appointment, my Dramatic Italian Lady Doctor reaches over to touch my arm, forcing me to stop writing and look at her. I explain that I can't concentrate without a pen in my hand. She insists I put down my pen and listen. After the appointment, I find a corner to sit down and record what she said, but I can't remember anything—my head started swimming the second she stopped me from taking notes.

But what is the point of all this note taking? Note-taking is not writing. Writing is about narrative and point of view. It needs a structure and a propulsiveness. My point of view is fractured. I don't know what my story is. I don't feel like a person with cancer. I know there are nodules and lesions and lumps in my thyroid, lungs, stomach, liver, abdomen, and lymph nodes, but they're not doing anything that affects me in any discernible way. Meanwhile, as the main character, I'm committing the worst sin possible—remaining a passive victim instead of an active party, wholly at the mercy of other people's decisions about my body.

I ask my writer friend Ian Brown to lunch to talk about writing. He's the one who, as a valued mentor, gave me the idea to write this book, and, as a man with the emotional wherewithal of a white male Boomer WASP, asked me if I was "taking notes" when he found out I had cancer, instead of sympathizing like a normal person. When we meet, a lot of our conversation is ridiculous—a ritualistic and highly enjoyable routine of talking about how hard writing is, and how we'll never figure it out because we're so useless, etc. But eventually I ask him, "So why do you write?" He sees I'm serious and switches from facetious to thoughtful. The real reason he writes, he says, "is to find out what I think."

I get that. Writing forces you to organize your research and your thoughts into a structure that makes sense of life's chaos. But as we keep talking, I realize there's another reason I write—which is that rare joy you sometimes get while working hard on a piece and then some force in the universe steps in and makes it better. I used to experience this phenomenon when I played sports—volleyball at university, then rowing for various clubs in Manitoba and Ontario. You train for months on end, put your heart and soul into a competition, and just when you think you're going to die trying, something clicks, and everything is suddenly smooth and beautiful instead of gut-wrenchingly hard. It's as if you're watching yourself compete and you want to laugh at how perfectly simple it is, and why can't it always be this way?

After my lunch with Brown, though, I still can't see how to structure a narrative out of my notes. Or even what tone to take. Should I aim for sad and profound? Or lighthearted and entertaining? I look up a quote from Hilary Mantel writing about Elizabeth Jean Howard: *Comedy is not generated by a writer who sails to her desk saying, "Now I will be funny." It comes from someone who crawls to her desk, leaking shame and despair, and begins to describe faithfully how things are. In that fidelity to the details of misery, one feels relish. The grimmer it is, the better it is: slowly, reluctantly, comedy seeps through.*

I definitely have details of misery. Like when I have a chest biopsy one morning and my lung collapses when I get home, sending me back to the hospital that afternoon. On the gurney in ER, the pain paralyzes me until the hydromorphone kicks in and I revert to my frantically jovial, suck-up mode with the ER doc. I find out he and his wife are both here from Ireland on fellowships, and he realizes it was his wife who did my biopsy that morning. "Hah!" I say. "The deadly Dublin duo!" I see him grimace through his mask. "That's a bit dark," he says. I rush to make amends: "I'm a TV writer! We're terrible people! We think in these macabre terms all the time!" He jams a giant aspirator needle into my chest, and I spend the next week in the hospital attached to a pump draining fluid off my lung.

Is this a funny story?

Or the night I can't sleep due to a painful inflammation in my hips and glutes so I get up and apply Tiger Balm over the entire area. But when it starts to sting, I suddenly remember I have a colonoscopy in the morning. I check out my burning backside in the mirror. I look like a baboon in heat. I jump into a cool shower and apply Aveeno oatmeal lotion to gently remove the Tiger Balm. The next morning, the doctor and nurse don't notice or don't care about any residual inflammation.

Is that a funny story?

When I try to write about these supposedly amusing events, I just start crying—a passive nonhero, stuck at her desk, leaking shame and despair.

4

David

Relationships in my life change. Some change subtly over time. Others change quickly, as with, for example, a long-time friend who repeatedly asks what preparations I've made for dying. I don't want to think about this yet. I think, *Why are we talking about me dying?* I decide to laugh it off. "I'm not ready to joke about it," I finally tell them. The person stiffens. "I wasn't joking," they reply, lips compressed, eyes narrowed. I start to apologize—and then it occurs to me: *Why am I appeasing this person for the millionth time in our relationship? I'm the one who has cancer.*

Another heady thought follows: *I don't have to put up with this anymore. Let the culling begin!*

In fact, I don't really start culling. But I do find it handy to have excuses—medical appointments, fear of germs, fatigue—to wiggle out of anything I don't want to do. It's also a relief to avoid a certain category of folks who thrive on malicious gossip and ancient grudges. I used to be in there like a dirty shirt, but now I find the negativity leaves me drained and itchy with disappointment at myself for passively enabling it.

But then I start avoiding my good friends, too. I don't know how to act around them. Do they expect me to talk about it? If I do talk about it, will I sound like a negative, complaining, self-involved asshole? Do I owe it to them to report medical details? I don't even understand my medical details. All I do is go for tests and scans with no treatment in sight. I decide to avoid the whole subject, but then I feel like I'm being coy—is there an elephant in the room, or is it just me? Also, when I do try to talk about other things, normal things, I can't concentrate. The scrolling newsfeed (*cancer, cancer, cancer, cancer*) in my mind's eye is too distracting.

There is one person I do want to talk to: David, my very first boyfriend, a semi-retired pathologist who teaches part-time at the University of Alberta in Edmonton. We've always kept in touch. He's been a major influence in my life, meaning more to me than I meant to him, I always thought, though I will later learn that maybe I'm wrong about this. I met him when I was fourteen, on Osborne Street in South Winnipeg. I was dressed in my St. Mary's Academy uniform, clutching schoolbooks to my flat chest, accompanied by my best friend Kimmy, a Protestant who went to school with boys, drank lemon gin on the weekends, and on that day was wearing Lee jeans and a gingham blouse whose buttons strained valiantly across her large bust. We ran into two boys she knew. I don't remember the other one. I had eyes only for David, the tallish, skinny one with messy brown hair and prescription horn-rimmed glasses with lenses that turned brown in the sunlight. They never really became clear, so he always looked a bit like a yellow-eyed serial killer.

A few weeks later, I ran into David again on Osborne. I was coming from my job at the library, where I worked after school as a "page," shelving books. It was spring, with darkness still falling early, and I was walking the gauntlet between the pool hall on the east side of Osborne and a greasy spoon called the Pit on the west side. There were always boys milling around each venue, places strictly verboten for me or any decent girl. You had to trot past quickly, eyes down, ignoring the leering predators as they lounged outside or dashed to and fro across Osborne.

David peeled off from the Pit group and caught up to me, asking if he could walk me home. I was thrilled. We began a conversation about movies, and I critiqued a film I'd seen on TV the night before, saying it had plot problems but otherwise was "free of flaws."

"Free of *flaws*?" he fake-exclaimed. "Then what on earth did they stand on?"

I'd never met anyone so smart or witty in my entire life.

Teenage dating for a Catholic-school virgin in the 1970s meant movies, walks down by the river, watching *Hawaii Five-O* with my siblings in the basement, or talking about schoolwork in the living room. Mostly, it was him talking and me asking questions like, "What is organic chemistry?" I still remember it has something to do with carbon, but I was more interested when he talked about physics and electrons, of which apparently there were an infinite number buzzing around the universe holding things together—or, as David pronounced dramatically one night, "Maybe there's just one electron, *but it's everywhere at the same time!*" This blew my mind. I still think about it.

I attended his grade-twelve prom, to which I wore no makeup and a long shirt dress buttoned to the neck that I'd sewn myself. Then we broke up, and I started going around with another boy. This one had long dark hair and wore a suede jacket with fringes that swung wildly as he strode around the neighborhood. He attended the University of Winnipeg, where he was on the fencing team, so I spent a lot of time listening to him talk about the differences between epées, foils, and sabers. For the first few weeks of our relationship, I remained a committed virgin. This changed after we attended a picnic for the fencing team at a park with a small lake outside the city.

I was younger than everyone else, a shy high schooler too self-conscious to change into my bathing suit. I sat with my knees hunched up on a towel on the grass while my boyfriend played frisbee and swam and drank beer with his university friends. Eventually, he flopped down beside me. He smiled at me with affection and slapped the side of my thigh in a gesture that I knew was half playful, half frustrated desire. Then he rolled over and sat up to watch the swimmers, which included a girl he was close friends with. I liked her too. She was cheerful and friendly, and curvy. When she rose out of the water, yanking up pieces of her tiny bikini as they got dragged down by the water, she looked like a wholesome, plumpish, Winnipeg version of Ursula Andress in *Dr. No.*

She brought over her towel and joined us. I watched my boyfriend watching her, and had two thoughts: One, if women were supposed to be skinny like Twiggy, then why wasn't she self-conscious about how her bikini barely covered her big, round bum and soft belly and large, jiggly bosom? And two, no matter how much my boyfriend might like me, he wasn't going to last much longer with a high schooler who refused to have sex.

But that's not why I decided to lose my virginity to him. I decided to lose my virginity because I wanted to be a writer, and you can't be a real writer if you've never experienced *life*. Since I knew I never wanted to get married, this meant I'd have to commit the mortal sin of having sex outside of marriage. Obviously, that meant eternal damnation, but if I really wanted to be a writer I could see no way around it.

You might argue that I could have sex and go to confession afterward to clear the debt and avoid Hell. But although I didn't believe in God, I respected his rules. Confession only works if you mean it. I knew when I had sex it wasn't going to be a moment of lustfully losing control, followed by anguished remorse and an urgent need to reinstate myself into God's good graces. I was going to have premeditated, unequivocally sinful sex, and what's more, I'd probably have sex with other people too, because isn't that what all good writers do? Muriel Spark, Doris Lessing, Beryl Bainbridge, Jean Rhys—these were my role models, brilliant writers who'd all had more than one liaison with men, usually to disastrous effect. But which, demonstrably, was an excellent source of material.

And so, one sunny summer day, off I went to the boyfriend's apartment, a rambling old red-brick apartment block on North Osborne, with the kind of spacious, unrenovated suites that were cheap to rent back then—endless large rooms, eat-in kitchen, original woodwork everywhere, dust motes floating in the late afternoon sun—and he cheerfully complied with my sudden change of heart, or head. Afterward, he assured me that "it's never good for girls the first time," spoken as one who'd never heard of the female orgasm, though I can hardly blame him, since I'd barely heard of it myself. I broke up with him a week or so later and refrained from dating anyone for the next year—no longer a virgin, but, having ticked it off my list, with no interest in sex either.

Until I ran into David one night at the University of Manitoba. I was coming from an event at the Student Union building. He was studying late with friends. We started talking, then wandered off down a dark hallway and started kissing. He led me into an empty classroom, and we had sex on the floor—after which I tearfully confessed that I'd already done it with another boy. "Thank God," he said. "Now I don't have to feel guilty."

David and I dated off and on for the next five years. No matter how many times we broke up, whenever we ran into each other we got back together. We finally broke up for good one night while walking home from a movie in downtown Winnipeg. We were cutting through the grounds of the Legislative Building and stopped to look at the original Louis Riel statue, which depicted him in the nude, twisted in agony. I loved it, but some in the Métis community objected to it as obscene and disrespectful, and it was later replaced by a more statesmanlike rendition of Riel, fully clothed and holding the Manitoba Act, which is a joke because the moment Manitoba joined Confederation in 1870, loathsome John A. Macdonald and his corrupt eastern cronies only betrayed and took advantage of the West. Riel led a resistance movement against them and was hanged for his troubles in 1885. Maybe that's what we started arguing about. David and I had virtually identical politics, but I was always more irked about everything. What I do remember are David's final words: "Call me when you know what you want!" Then he turned on his heel and walked away from me. We both left Winnipeg soon after that, him to England, then Edmonton, and me to Toronto. We met other people, had children, and ended up separated and single again in our fifties.

But as I said, we never lost touch. We wrote letters and Christmas cards back in the day, then started emailing, and then texting. I'd be making coffee and send him a grumbly message about how long it took: *Every time I make filter coffee I stand here like an idiot doing ten little pours because you told me in high school that many small infusions make a stronger brew.* Then he'd text back: *I haven't used a comb since 1978 because you told me to use my fingers instead.* Then we'd ignore each other for another six or twelve or eighteen months. On big birthdays or Christmases, we'd exchange woolen socks or cashmere sweaters.

There was an awkward period in 2015, when I decided we should get married. Part of me always truly believed we'd end up together. But I also had ulterior motives: I wanted to marry David in order to punish K.F., another, more recent ex. I had a long, messy relationship with K.F. years earlier. We are still friends. But for years after our breakup, he maintained a delusional fantasy that it was a mistake (it was not) and someday we'd reunite. But first he had to deal with his ex-wife, not to mention his current live-in girlfriend, whom he spoke of as someone who'd mysteriously obtained keys to his house and was now immovably living there. The situation came to a head during lunch with another friend, who told me that K.F. had just been on holiday with his girlfriend, but it was a big secret in case his ex-wife or I found out.

I could barely get through the rest of lunch; I was so angry at being cast as a desperate ex-lover in K.F.'s sociopathic 1950s fantasy of the beleaguered playboy pursued by a posse of lovelorn women. Walking home from the restaurant on that miserable, grey Toronto day, my anger was exacerbated further by the big, wide-legged, grey woolen trousers I was wearing, which kept twisting around my legs in the wind, making me stumble and curse every few steps.

Then, in the distance, as if my rage had conjured him up, there he was: K.F., walking toward me. With a genius for negging and an infallible radar for my insecurities around possible fashion mistakes, he started wagging his finger at my baggy grey pants from half a block away. By the time he reached me, all I could do was watch his lips move, unable to hear anything over the raging wind outside and the raging turmoil inside my head.

I interrupted him. “I’m getting married.”

There are moments in life when an event unfolds like a Hollywood movie, perfect in execution and result. This was one of those moments. His jaw dropped. His tongue practically rolled out and hit the sidewalk like Wile E. Coyote’s.

“To who?” he croaked.

“My very first boyfriend. We met when I was fourteen. He was my first love, and I guess I just never stopped loving him as ‘the one,’ you know? Anyway, he lives out west, but we’ve always stayed in touch, and it just became obvious that we’re meant to be together.”

“What about our relationship?”

I patted his arm. “Don’t worry,” I said kindly. “Our relationship will be fine! We’ll stay friends, *like we are now*.”

Leaving him stunned and silent, I continued on home in

a much better mood. Even my stupid pants calmed down and stopped trying to kill me. I thought about how, throughout my relationship with K.F., I'd always been the honest, long-suffering, faithful partner, and he'd been the cheating, lying, dishonest bastard. *What a mistake*, I thought. *I should've been lying this whole time. Lying is awesome!*

Even better, I technically hadn't lied. I really did still love David. We really had stayed in touch all these years. And who's to say we wouldn't get married? Did he, or did he not say to me, "Call me when you know what you want"? Well, I do know, sir. I want to be your wedded wife, and now is the time.

I called Air Canada and booked a flight to Edmonton. Conveniently, I was working on a project set in Alberta that would benefit from local, tax-deductible research, so I booked interviews with cops, mining people, and a sociologist at the university where David was working and teaching.

Everything started off according to plan. I embarked on my interviews on day one, then met up with David at the University of Alberta on the second day for a drink at the faculty club. He seemed a bit . . . circumspect. I'd forgotten how long he'd known me, and how well. Did he suspect something was up? But he readily agreed to a dinner date the next evening.

He picked me up at my hotel and took me to a nice restaurant where I immediately got drunk, while he abstained as the designated driver. During dessert, fearing things were going too slowly, I reached over to touch the arm of his soft cashmere blazer, and suggested we continue our date back at my hotel.

His arm shot up. "Check, please." But a moment later, he said, "In the interests of full disclosure, I should tell you I have a girlfriend."

I punched his cashmere-clad arm. "Then why on earth did you let me get drunk and flirt with you like a complete idiot?"

He lifted his arms in a giant doofus-male shrug. "Well, she's actually married, so . . ."

Great. Just what I needed. An entanglement with another man semi-involved with another woman. With nothing to lose, I told him my plan to entrap him into marriage. He reacted the way he reacts to everything—phlegmatically. "Look, we live half a country apart and neither of us is going to move." Fine. I then revealed my ulterior motive, i.e., my revenge plot against the ex-boyfriend in Toronto. "I told him you were my very first boyfriend and that we finally got engaged after all these years."

David nodded. "Okay."

"So if you ever come to Toronto to visit me, can you pretend to be my fiancé?"

He nodded again. "I can absolutely do that."

Back in Toronto, as months went by without me announcing any nuptials, K.F. grew suspicious. When we met on the street one day, he outright accused me: "I think this fiancé of yours is a complete fiction." Taking a page from his old playbook, I responded with indignation. "Of course he exists!

These things take time! I love him! We were just texting this morning! We're thinking of eloping to Paris! You know how much I love Paris!" I ended my rant with a smile. *Who's the shameless, transparent, duplicitous liar now, asshole?* (I don't know what it says about the two of us, but somehow we have stayed close friends through all these shenanigans.)

In the seven years following this episode, David and I stayed in touch as much as ever, though I was careful not to overstep in case he thought I was still trying to entrap him. So now, calling to tell him I have cancer, I feel self-conscious about appearing manipulative or exploitive. The call begins with me saying hello, then bursting into tears, which makes my voice go all squeaky. He suggests I call him back in twenty minutes when I've stopped squeaking—which instantly stops my tears: "It's talking to you that's making me squeak, you idiot," I say. "Waiting twenty minutes won't make any difference."

I tell him my news. He doesn't say *Omigod*, or *I'm so sorry*, or *what can I do*? He just listens, phlegmatically, which is exactly what I want. I ask him questions and take notes as he starts talking:

- Cells constantly dividing
- If a cell mutates and doesn't get discarded, then a second mutation
- DNA fucked up when replicating
- Possible to catch it in time—e.g., mutations produce one polyp, no problem, remove it before the second mutation

- . . . apoptosis . . . suicide path . . . immune system is stupid . . . it attacks the cells . . . T-cells . . .
- ??? different genotypes in one tumor ??? heterogeneity in tumors because they can't repair themselves
- There's no way of knowing how or when it started: a cell can mutate and sit there for years, then another mutation happens and it starts proliferating

David tells me to call him anytime. I'm careful not to bother him too often but fall gratefully into a pattern of calling every few weeks to ask medical questions, such as how to interpret the jargon in CT scan results—which I carefully strip clean of embarrassing content, like the amount of fecal matter in my colon. Except one time I forget to do this, and start apologizing. He doesn't care. He launches into an anecdote about the scan results of a prominent national newspaper columnist "who shall remain nameless," and how the radiologist was telling him about the eminent personality's "considerable fecal load." David had dearly wanted to reply, "I couldn't agree with you more, sir," but refrained.

Our conversations are not always about my medical condition. One night after I get a scan that is full of more bad news, I call him after I've gone to bed. But when I hear his voice, I don't want to talk about cancer. I just want to listen in the dark while he drones on about himself and his life in Edmonton. He complies, while I quietly weep at how familiar his voice is—he sounds exactly like the sixteen-year-old David talking about organic chemistry and electrons. He tells me about his two German short-haired pointers, Zena and Hazel; the various states of repair of all his bicycles; the lamentable, fatal, elitist arrogance of Rachel Notley's NDP party, whom he always votes for anyway. One of the few subjects that rouses him from his usual dispassionate affect is celebrity scientist Neil deGrasse Tyson: "He's always saying that science explains everything! It does not! It's only the best approximation of reality we have at the moment with given proofs so far!" Mind you, he adds, "You better hope Newtonian physics are true when you press the brake pedal on your car."

A few months later, I bring up a question I've been too afraid or too ashamed to ask: "How did I get cancer?" By which I mean: *Is it my fault I have cancer?*

He gives me his usual caveat that even though he's seen thousands of cancer slides as a pathologist, he's retired, and his knowledge is out of date, and the entire field has changed in the past five years, and I tell him I don't care. "You know more than I do—just tell me what you think." So he starts talking, and I take fast and not always accurate notes; this is a precise transcription:

- Maybe thirty years ago a melanocyte in my skin had a mutation that changed an x-acine to thymacine to another-cine . . .
- The code/blueprint for the body, DNA for different molecules ACTP . . . encodes Ellen Vanstone, gets three in a

row . . . codon . . . amino acid . . . agc glycine . . . tta ph . . . building blocks for protein encoded in Ribosomes read msg stripped off the DNA

- Random event set off mutation then poss a second event . . .
- I ate a steak containing a carcinogenic molecule that some cow ate . . .
- I walked too close to a radioactive source . . . a deposit of uranium . . . a radon spat at me

He ends with a shrug: "Maybe it was a cosmic event." I take this to mean he's referring to the actions of a Vengeful God who gave me cancer to punish me for my years of sin and slutitude. Which makes total sense to me.

But a few weeks later, when I mention that I assumed he meant "cosmic event" as a kind of joke or metaphor, he emphatically corrects me. "First," he says, "there's not a goddamn thing you could've done to prevent it. It's completely random."

Second, he meant "cosmic event" literally. "We live in a soup of cosmic rays," he says. "Airline pilots are drenched in them." He tells me that my cancer could have been triggered by a gamma ray from a quasar in a distant galaxy. "It could have come from the dawn of the universe when the Big Bang sent out a photon that passed through one of the nucleotide bases in your DNA."

I like this explanation. I start to feel less guilty about

getting cancer. I relax as David goes off on a tangent about how the photon that went from the Big Bang 13.8 billion years ago to my groin in 2022 "would not have experienced any passage of time at all."

"Because Einstein, right?" I say.

Yes, he says. "A photon has no mass; it has to move at the speed of light. And as Einstein showed, when you near the speed of light, time slows down."

Then he tells me a joke: Heisenberg, Schrödinger, and Ohm are on a road trip, and they get pulled over. Heisenberg is driving and the cop asks him, "Do you know how fast you were going?"

"No, but I know exactly where I am," Heisenberg replies.

The cop says, "You were going eighty miles an hour."

Heisenberg throws up his hands and shouts, "Great! Now I'm lost!"

The cop thinks this is suspicious and orders him to pop open the trunk, then says, "Do you know you have a dead cat back here?"

"Well, I do now, asshole!" shouts Schrödinger.

The cop tries to arrest them. Ohm resists.

I still think he is the wittiest, smartest boy I know.

5

Treatment

Throughout the summer, things keep happening to me—tests, scans, and biopsies, the drama of a collapsed lung. I thought that by this time, I'd be bravely enduring chemo treatments, wanly accepting food and attention from a rotation of devoted friends, losing my hair. I'd even picked out a wig—a platinum blonde bob, unapologetically fake but still cool, a cross between Carol Channing and Sia.

But after two months at Cancer Care Manitoba, then another two months at Princess Margaret, nothing is happening treatment-wise. I have a lump in my left inguinal lymph node, plus nodes, nodules, and lesions in my stomach, lungs, liver, and abdomen, along with a dense but stable mass beside my "vaginal vault." (I gather that "vaginal vault" simply means vagina, but I like this term and will use it exclusively from now on to refer to that honored part of my anatomy.)

But I feel perfectly fine, the same as before I was diagnosed. I don't need meals or handholding from my friends, and wonder if I'm disappointing everyone by not being more pathetic. Finally, in July, my doctor tells me they're going to start me on immunotherapy injections of ipilimumab and nivolumab every three weeks, for a total of four treatments over twelve weeks.

I think I understand the basics: whereas chemotherapy basically poisons you in hopes of poisoning the cancer cells as well, immunotherapy boosts the immune system so it will attack cancer cells. There's a risk of the invigorated immune system attacking everything else, potentially triggering inflammatory autoimmune conditions like colitis, arthritis, bursitis, skin conditions, and so forth. One thing it does not typically cause is baldness, so I won't lose my hair and get to wear a cool wig, but that's fine. At least I can expect a predictable schedule of hospital visits, followed by scans that will give definitive information about whether it worked or not.

I find it slightly confusing when they talk about side effects as opposed to "irAEs: IO-related" effects, meaning "immune-related adverse events." Aren't "side" effects and "adverse" effects the same thing? But I don't sweat it. I decide that with enough willpower, I will avoid all of the above.

Friends offer to come with me for my treatments. But I prefer to go alone so I don't have to play hostess at the cancer factory and feel guilty about taking up their whole day. And it does take almost a whole day. After check-in on the fourth floor, you carry around a big old-fashioned pager, and wait two to three hours until it blasts off with vibrations and an ear-splitting electronic beep that sends you racing from the second-floor piano lounge or the main-floor food court back up to the fourth floor, where they turn off the pager and assign you to a pod in the color-coordinated treatment bays—Orange 17 or Purple 23, etc.

Once ensconced in your pod, you wait another hour or so, while a nurse takes your vitals and gives you Benadryl and Tylenol in case of allergic or pain reactions to the infusion. Finally, they bring the drugs, and the nurse calls out for a colleague to come and double-check the label on the bag, making sure it matches the label on my wrist. Then they triple-check it all with me, making me state my name, birthdate, and medical records number to make sure I'm the right recipient. I heard a story when I was a little kid about a guy going in for surgery and the doctor amputating the wrong leg, which makes me terrified someone is going to cut off one of my legs by mistake at some point, so I very much appreciate all the caution.

Everyone is incredibly patient and nice. On the second visit, when it seems more crowded than the first, I ask the reception nurse why. She says they usually get 300 patients per day, but for a variety of reasons, the number today is a thousand. "We don't turn anyone away." I ask her if she wants me to stand up and announce: *Everyone who voted for Doug Ford, please go to the back of the line!* I've made this joke before with mixed results, but this time I get a smile.

Inside the pod, I ask the injection nurse why it takes so long between checking in and getting the injection. I don't mind, of course! I'm merely curious. She explains that each infusion costs $40,000 so they don't like to "mix it all together" before making sure the patient is present, willing, and able.

My willpower is obviously working, because after three treatments over July and August, I am still free of any pesky side effects. So when I get a call from Tim, a Disney TV location manager who offers me $24,000 to vacate my condo for nine days in September so they can shoot scenes for a TV pilot in my dining room, I think about my unemployed status and say yes. On top of the fee, Tim says they will also pay for an Airbnb, which turns out to be a cute ground-floor unit in a renovated house near Christie Pits park.

But when I show up at the unit, there's no key in the lockbox. Then, the door flies open and I'm met by a young woman wearing only a t-shirt and panties. She screams when she sees me: "I'm sorry! I spilled something on my pants! I'm not finished cleaning the unit! Check-in time is 4 p.m.!"

She slams the door in my face. I check my emails and confirm that she is wrong. Check-in time is 3 p.m. But there's nothing I can do. I leave my luggage in my car and wander around for an hour. When I return, the woman is gone but the floors are sticky and there are two giant, used Q-tips covered in a prodigious amount of earwax beside the bathroom sink. I take a picture of the Q-tips and send it to the host, who sends back an abject apology. Then I wash the floors, sterilize the kitchen and bathroom, and settle down on the couch to watch TV for the next nine days.

Then, there's a pain in my abdomen that feels unlike anything I've experienced before. I ignore it. But a few hours later, when I'm doubled over with pain and burning up with fever, I call my niece Ruth, and she drives me to the hospital. It's my first of many visits to the ER over the next three years. When I go to check in, the intercom doesn't work. An utterly defeated woman behind the Covid-proof, possibly bulletproof glass repeatedly asks me questions, while I repeatedly yell back at her—*What? Pardon? What?*—because the intercom doesn't work.

Eventually, the ER reception nurse gets up and sticks her head out of the glass door beside her cubicle. I give her my information. I'm triaged by a harried nurse who sticks a needle in my arm to take blood, then jumps up to deal with a ruckus outside the door. When she comes back I have blood all down my arm, on my pants, on the floor, which I'm mopping up with a paper towel. "Ah, you're a bleeder, eh?" she says. Then she runs out again.

I find some tape and gauze to dress the wound, and then press down on it to stop the bleeding. I go back to sit in the waiting room, where I pass out from the pain. When I awake they're wheeling me through the door and into an ER hallway to wait for the oncologist on duty. He shows up hours later, apologizing that they don't have a bed available for me so I'm stuck in the hallway for now. I don't care. I'm so distracted by pain, and so intent on getting a shot of hydromorphone, it doesn't matter where I am.

On the third day, they find a bed for me and I'm wheeled up to a ward containing four other patients, including a woman across from me who's in very bad shape. She's refusing to have her vitals taken or to drink or eat anything, snapping and swearing at the nurses to leave her alone. The nurses never stop being kind and patient with her, which makes me want to jump up and scold her for being so mean. But I'm too tired to move. Then I overhear a conversation about what she's been through: endless chemo, side effects, infections, and a blood disease. "I'm garbage," she keeps saying. "Just throw me out. I want to die." That night, groggy with drugs but constantly awakened by her groans and the nurses who come in regularly to check on her, I'm completely on her side. I consider going over to talk to her, to find out if she really wants to end it all, which makes perfect sense to me, and if there's any way I can help her.

In the morning, I wake up and she's still there. Her husband and daughter are visiting, the daughter trying to persuade her to cooperate and take her medicine. The husband is on the phone, talking to someone at his work. He's tall, with thick silver hair and a beaky nose. He looks like Samuel Beckett. His job sounds like something in construction or maybe maintenance at some large outfit like Toronto public transit. "I'm not in the office till later," he says at one point. "The wife's not too well." His old-fashioned stoicism makes me want to cry. I recall my plan from the night before, to sneak over to the woman's bed with a pillow and put her out of her misery, and am relieved I didn't follow through. I doubt the authorities would understand. I wonder if they'd still give me immunotherapy treatments if I was in jail, and then they give me more hydromorphone and I fall asleep again.

I'm diagnosed with transaminitis, meaning the immunotherapy has riled up my liver enzymes. They want to keep me for longer. Luckily, my friend Johanna has dropped off a giant tin of snickerdoodles, and I offer one to the doctor doing rounds. He rubs his tiny paunch and says he shouldn't. But then he takes one and wolfs it down. We continue to discuss whether I should be discharged while I feed him more snickerdoodles. I fill a sterile biohazard bag with half a dozen more for him. He finally agrees to let me go home.

I go back to the Airbnb, which is now clean and tidy, but I'm desperate to get back into my condo and can hardly wait the two more days I'm stuck here. Then I get a text from Tim the location manager: *We might need an extra day.* I know the film business, so I know he's lying through his teeth, and really means several extra days. And he knows I know. I reply: *Tim, you are a lying bastard.* He texts back: *lol I know!*

I have trouble sleeping in the Airbnb and wander out at dawn to walk along Bloor Street toward Christie Pits. In the heat, the street smells of stale beer and cigarette butts, the dregs of another night of revelry by the locals. I don't mind. I'm wearing a t-shirt and jeans, neither of which fit properly because I've lost so much weight. My arms are skeletal, covered in bruises from IV lines, blood collection lines, and veins that refused to yield to the needle. As I walk along, unsteadily veering as I lose my balance in the bright light, I think of other ashen-faced, skeletal, staggering characters I've seen on these streets, in clothes that don't fit, veering left and right, with arms showing bruises and track marks. I think to myself: Perhaps I have judged these people too harshly in the past.

I make my way down into the park and stop to rest at a picnic table covered in drawings of penises. They're all circumcised. I wonder if graffiti in England features penises with big, floppy foreskins. I don't understand what motivates people to do this, but I'm not offended. The penises look quite jaunty and festive. The sun is rising and the park is ridiculously picturesque—lush green grass over rolling wee hillocks. Life is good.

Until I go back to the Airbnb and ear-splitting fire alarms start going off throughout the day. I call the host, who sends an electrician, who manages to turn off the alarm but says it's a Band-Aid fix and the whole house needs to be rewired. Moments after he leaves, the alarms go off again. Fire trucks come. They send me outside while they do an inspection and silence the alarms. A few hours of silence follow—until 9 p.m., when they start going off again. By 11 p.m., I am packed and out the door. I drive back to my condo. Fuck Tim the location manager—I'll camp out in my bedroom at the back of my unit while they finish shooting in the front rooms. But when I get there, my bedroom is filled with bags and boxes and racks of wardrobe items, and my whole condo reeks like a rotting vintage shop permeated with mildew and body odor.

It's after midnight when I put on my knapsack, exit my condo, and start walking down Spadina Road. It's been raining and the streets are mostly empty and gleaming under the streetlights. I feel like I'm on a movie set, where they wet the pavement for exterior street scenes to make everything look prettier. I try to act the part—a brave woman with a dire disease walking through the night with nowhere to go.

In fact, I have plenty of places to go. I could call any one of my friends to take me in. But I'm too tired and demoralized to face explaining everything. I still haven't learned how to ask for help. I'm going to win the stoicism trophy if it kills me.

So I keep walking, reminding myself that I'm in no real danger. I live in a safe neighborhood. I am a privileged elderly lady. I have a phone and a credit card in my pocket.

And indeed, by the time I've walked the two blocks from Kendal to Bloor, I've found a hotel room around the corner at the Kimpton Saint George. The cheapest rooms start at $800, which shocks my out-of-date brain because I've gone absolutely nowhere since before Covid.

But I'm not worried. Tim the lying bastard can pay.

2023

6
Drug Trials

After the attack of transaminitis, my doctor tells me immunotherapy is no longer an option. The adverse effects are too severe: inflammation in various joints and organs, along with a case of colitis that requires 100 mg of Prednisone per day to stop my insides from liquifying into one, long, endless bout of diarrhea. I learn that 100 mg is a high dose when one of the doctors I see during my near-daily visits to PMH exclaims in horror: "Are you sure it's 100 mg per day?!" Yup. I'm also getting infusions of something called Infliximab, along with IV hydration, hydromorphone for pain, and anti-nausea meds. To add insult to injury, I learn that these side effects won't disappear now that I'm off treatment. Thanks to my super-activated immune system, there will be a permanent, disabling feature of my life going forward. I feel like someone should apologize for this, but no one ever does.

The good news is that Dr. S., my Dramatic Italian Lady Doctor, is looking for a clinical trial whereby an experimental new treatment might help me. I learn that Princess Margaret has approximately 350 trials going on at any given time so there's plenty to choose from.

Except that I'm "atypical." My melanoma is of "unknown origin"—they have now designated it as the "mucosal" variety because it probably originated in my vulva, though there's been no evidence of it there (another sick joke from my Vengeful God; pretty unsubtle if you ask me), which is on the rarer side, plus I have an "atypical BRAF mutation variant Gly469Ala."

At first I think being atypical is good: I'm special! I'll get more attention! But it only makes it harder for Dr. S. to find a study I'm eligible for. She tells me not to use the word "colitis," for instance, when I'm filling out the endless questionnaires that come with applying for any of the trials. "Just say you have diarrhea"—a fib that might make me eligible for the study she wants me in.

This is a signal moment for me. I go from thinking I'm a nameless, disposable nobody that my terrifying Dramatic Italian Lady Doctor only sees as fodder for experimental drug trials, to loving her for looking out for me. Which she does over and over. When I need an endoscopy, colonoscopy, sigmoidoscopy, eye exam, or any other procedure as part of a screening for a trial, I always get in immediately—to the point where one doctor shakes his head at having to squeeze me into his schedule. "The only reason you got in today is because of Dr. S. She really fights for her patients," he grumbles. When I thank a trial nurse for her over-and-above treatment of me during one visit, she says, "Dr. S. told me you're a protected patient." I ask if "protected patient" is a medical term. No, she says, "It's just how Dr. S. refers to you."

And so, in due course, my champion, Dr. S. finds a drug trial for me—albeit an unfortunately named one, the BEAVER study, their acronym for "Binimetinib and Encorafenib for the treatment of Advanced solid tumors with non-V600E BRAF mutations." It involves taking nineteen giant capsules a day of Encorafenib and Binimetinib. The giant capsules make me sick from the second I manage to swallow all nineteen of them down. After a few days I start vomiting and they tell me to stop the pills. Then I go back for an assessment and then I try again. It keeps happening. They reduce the dose. They delete one set of pills. I still get sick.

Every time I start a new course, I feel like Charlie in *Flowers for Algernon*, waving "bye-bye, world" as a blanket of vomitus ineptitude once again encloses my brain. I've already gone from 135 to 105 pounds; now I lose another five pounds practically overnight. I'm frail. When my dog knocks me over at the dog park, I break two ribs and cannot get up until a neighbor—Dog Park Peter, as I come to call him—stops laughing at me and realizes I need help.

After three months of experimenting with reduced dosages, Dr. S. calls it quits on the BEAVER trial and starts looking for another one. Soon I'm in the much better-named ARTISTRY-6 phase 2 trial. The routine on this one is five straight days of injections every three weeks, with each infusion followed by several hours of observation, during which I routinely throw up and start convulsing with "rigors," a new word for me, meaning violent shivering that can turn into convulsions and kill you if left untreated. The nurses who monitor me in the brand-new Convergence Centre for drug-trial patients know how to get a needle into me ASAP and start pumping me full of hydromorphone, Demerol, and Gravol until I stop vomiting and convulsing and am well enough to be sent home.

After a few months, Dr. S. takes me off the ARTISTRY-6 study, telling me the side effects are too onerous, and it's not working in any case. At this point, I'm almost two years into my cancer experience (or "journey," if you insist), consisting of exploration to confirm the diagnosis of stage-four melanoma, half a year of useless immunotherapy treatment, and now a year of drug trials that aren't working. The good news is that the disease isn't progressing, but the side effects have been deleterious, to say the least. The last episode involved me collapsing on my way into Princess Margaret before they even injected the dose. An emergency CT scan reported the presence of an "omental infarction." What on Earth is an "omental infarction"? It sounded like a punchline in a hospital sketch. My trial nurse, M.A.C., visits my bedside to see how I'm doing. She is about my age, and over the past year and dozens of appointments, we've gotten to know each other, talking about movies (she's obsessed with celebrities), the state of her marriage (not great), and other patients of hers who have died. She's never ruffled. Intrigued by the omental infarction development, she visits my pod, leans against the partition, folds her arms, and shakes her head at me. "You're so atypical."

At a subsequent visit, M.A.C. stands by while Dr. S. pulls up a chair to discuss options post-ARTISTRY-6. My manner with her has always been cheerful and talkative: *I'm nice! I'm friendly! Like me! Please don't cut off the wrong leg or kill me!* But there's something about her grave manner today that punctures my defenses. It's like when Nicole from Cancer Care Manitoba got all rattled on the phone about the malignant melanoma diagnosis and cued me to realize things might be more serious than I thought. My eyes fill with tears as Dr. S. talks, which makes her throw up her hands and exclaim: "Why are you crying? What do you think? You came to us with stage-four malignant melanoma! You have to look at the glass half full! You've already exceeded your prognosis!"

Excuse me? What prognosis? Nobody told me. Shit. The only prognosis I ever got is when one of her fellows told me that people with my kind of cancer have a forty percent chance of surviving five years, which I took to mean that the other sixty percent live longer than five years, which sounded like pretty good odds to me.

The good thing about Dr. S.'s dramatic exasperation with me, which I now understand is her way of showing care and concern, is that it bucks me up. I ask her what death looks like with my kind of cancer. She resists at first: "Why do you ask this? Why do you not stay positive?" But I need to have a scenario so I can prepare. So she explains that death could result from any number of causes: growth of tumors that cause organ failure; respiratory problems from the nodules in my lungs; liver failure from the growing lesions on that organ; heart failure as a side effect of organ failure. I don't find this comforting exactly. But it's definitely better than the endings I've been imagining—e.g., my enlarged liver bursting out of my abdomen like the baby monster in *Alien* while I scream in agony and everyone around me gets spattered in red-jello cancer cells.

Our conversation concludes with her repeating that I will still have to live with all the side effects—colitis, arthritis, bursitis, muscle cramps, anemia—I've acquired so far. But "the goal is to prolong life, as long as there is quality of life." Then she asks if I'm open to starting a new drug trial right away. It means another round of tests for my eligibility, starting with taking twenty vials of blood that day. I agree to everything.

After Dr. S. leaves the exam room, M.A.C. stays behind, presumably to offer moral support as I sit huddled in my chair, clutching fistfuls of damp tissues. As ever, she's fond of pointing out to me that we're all going to die. "The only difference between you and me," she says, "is that you have more information."

Dr. S. finds a trial that will take me: DS1055-A-J101, "A Phase 1, First In Human Study Of Ds-1055a In Subjects With Relapsed

Or Refractory Locally Advanced Or Metastatic Solid Tumors." I learn that "Phase 1" means the drugs have never been tested on humans. This makes me wonder about the poor little rabbits or rats or mice or monkeys who have been given cancer, then tortured with all these drugs before they got to me. I ask a cancer researcher I meet in the dog park if they work with animals at Princess Margaret. He refuses to answer: "That information is classified."

The DS1055 trial ends up being a breeze in terms of no side effects. Unfortunately, it annihilates my hemoglobin, iron levels, and so forth, which means interrupting the study to undergo various transfusions and injections. At one point, the ulcerated mass in my stomach goes haywire and they stop the trial so I can go in for five days of radiation. Then, a growing tumor in my groin calls for more radiation, and then palliative surgery to keep it in check. When I start having dizzy spells, they order an MRI that reveals a brain tumor—which calls for gamma-knife radiation to my head. For that procedure, they press a steaming hot sheet of polymer to my face to form a custom-made mask, which they use to bolt my head to the table so I can't move one single millimeter while the gamma-knife rays are shot into my brain. I concentrate on how amazing this technology is and ask the technician to take pictures with my iPhone, which I think could be fun and interesting to post on Instagram. But when I look at the photos later, they're not amazing. My pale face underneath the green mesh polymer looks wan and frightened. I delete all the images.

When various scans show the disease is still progressing, Dr. S. takes me off the DS1055 trial and puts me on another trial: a Phase 1/1b Open-label, Multicenter Clinical Study of MK-0472 as Monotherapy and Combination Therapy in Participants with Advanced/Metastatic Solid Tumors.

Whatever. I now regard going to the hospital three to five days every week as my job. I'm still dealing with side effects—which means multiple visits to the ER at Toronto General and occasional stays. There's always a lot going on in the ER waiting room. Like eight white cops who come in with a slim young Black woman wearing sweats. I sit up. My *Diggstown* writing brain stirs. What if they're mistreating her? What will I do? I close my eyes to think. When I open them again, there are only two cops, and one of them is telling the young woman to call them if she needs anything. She thanks him and follows a nurse through the glass doors into the ER, ahead of the rest of us who've been waiting for hours. Maybe she's a celebrity, but I don't recognize her, which means nothing because I don't know who anyone is anymore.

On another visit, I lie on a gurney in an ER hallway, listening to a young man behind the curtain next to me, hurling obscenities at the nurses and yelling for a "real nurse" and a "real doctor" to come and see him. After two days of this, I get off my gurney and charge into his space: "You're not the only one in pain here!" I yell at him. Unfortunately, it's not that satisfying. He's sitting with his mother and they both look up at me, startled and scared. I have a similar experience with another male patient on another hospital stay. I'm in a room with six beds. There are only supposed to be five, so my bed is in a corner surrounded by old lockers and discarded furniture. I can hear an old man at the other end of the room who never shuts up. He's either yelling at his visiting relatives, or yelling at the nurses, or ignoring his cellphone, constantly going off with the Italian national anthem. When he makes his own calls, he yells into the phone, hurling abuse at whomever he's talking to. By the third day, I've had enough. His phone goes off and I crawl unsteadily out of bed to make my way down the length of the room to confront him. To tell him what a selfish prick he is. To demand he turn off his stupid cellphone. When I get to his bed, he's lying with his body twisted, face to the window, completely out of it. He's small, skeletal, with a few strands of hair limp across his shiny skull, his eyes closed, his face in a grimace. Goddammit. I turn around and creep back to my own bed.

Aside from these ER and hospital stays, I cannot complain. On all my visits to the trial drug teams, I'm treated like royalty—like a glorified lab monkey, which is fine—the drug companies have a vested interest in keeping my anonymized carcass up and running, so I don't suddenly go blind or die and skew their results. During pre-treatment screening days, requiring hours of waiting for blood test results and a physical exam, I zone out in the shiny, new research clinic on the eighteenth floor. After treatments, I'm given warm blankets and ice water, and various medications to treat my pain or nausea or rigors, in the new Convergence Centre with its roomy pods and clean washrooms. The drug companies pay for all my Ubers to and from the hospital.

The trouble is, I'm still a passive character. An angry victim instead of a stoic hero. I need to take control over some aspect of my life, but what?

I decide to write some letters.

7

Anger

TO: Dr.—, dermatologist, Winnipeg

Dear Dr.—,

After seeing you precisely one time in 2020, when you looked at a suspected basal-cell carcinoma on my forehead and declared it benign, I called your office again to book another medical appointment. As I told your receptionist on the phone, I had just been diagnosed with stage-four metastatic melanoma and needed an overall basic skin check.

At this point, a normal human being might say something like, "I'm sorry to hear that," or, "I can definitely book an appointment for you right away." Instead, your receptionist ignored what I'd said and launched into a sales pitch for your cosmetic clinic, asking if I wanted "to book any cosmetic procedures."

I repeated my request for a medical appointment. He repeated his question as to whether I wanted to book a cosmetic procedure. I got the distinct impression that if I didn't book a cosmetic procedure, I could forget about booking any kind of medical appointment.

I gave up and went to a different dermatologist.

Now, two years later, to add insult to injury, I am still receiving your greed-induced marketing emails no matter how diligently I unsubscribe, or block them, or report them as spam.

Today I received yet another email from you offering "Ultherapy" treatments to "lift the neck, chin, and brow while improving lines and wrinkles on the upper chest," starting at $999.

The treatment promises a "fresher, more youthful look."

Please note that the only treatment I'm interested in now is for a "cancer-surviving, not-dead look."

Stop sending me these bullshit emails, you greedy POS.

Sincerely, etc.

TO: T—, Ministry of Health

CC: M—, N—, Minister Christine Elliott, Ministry of Health

Dear T—,

I was walking my dog to the park the other night at about 6 p.m. when my phone rang. Imagine my surprise when the caller identified herself as my Esteemed Italian Lady Doctor from Lake Como, who is the head of my oncology team at Princess Margaret Hospital. Note that I was crossing Bathurst Street in the dark on a very short pedestrian walk signal, and in my shock at hearing her voice, I almost dropped my phone, which would have been disastrous, as I was wearing a black coat and my labradoodle is black so we were virtually invisible. Drivers on Bathurst blast through groups of pedestrians day and night, so we'd have surely been run over if I'd had to stop and fish around on the pavement in the dark for my device.

In any case, I managed to hang on to my phone and make it across the street in one piece, where I waited with bated breath to see why my doctor was calling. She'd never called me before. It was after hours. Had she suddenly come across test results that predicted a sudden change in my prognosis? Was she calling to tell me I had miraculously conquered the army of metastases blooping in and around all my organs? Or was she calling to tell me to get my affairs in order because the news was bad, very bad, like six-weeks-to-live bad?

But no, T—, the reason my doctor was calling was to tell me she had my Entocort prescription expenses form in hand, but that she was unable to process it because Entocort—which costs me over $500 a month—is not covered under the "limited use" category or the "Exceptional Access Program" or the "Ontario Drug Benefit Program" or the "Trillium Drug

Program" or any other rabbit holes you sent me chasing down over the past year.

Now I ask you, T—, do you think it's a good use of this Esteemed Italian Lady Doctor's time—an individual who is one of the top cancer researchers in Canada, the recipient of national and international awards—to pore over the expense forms you sent me that are actually the wrong forms and should never have been sent to me at all? In fact, I just received a letter from another Ministry department telling me Entocort "is currently not funded for the requested indication," i.e., the drug is covered for only certain applications, and my application does not qualify.

Just to be clear, dear (I trust I may call you "dear," since you felt free to repeatedly call me "dear" in our most recent phone call), my situation is not good. I have tumors and lesions and nodules in my lymph nodes, lungs, liver, brain, abdomen, and an ulcerated mass in my stomach. My immune-related adverse effects include cataracts, persistent anemia, crippling arthritis, bursitis, transaminitis, and a case of colitis that requires a lifelong maintenance treatment of the drug in question, Entocort. Not to mention chronic leg cramps. My calves seize up every time I go for a dog walk. I have to stick close to lamp posts and hedges so I have something to hang on to when my legs stop working. I can't stray too far from my home in case of a sudden colitis attack requiring a swift return to my bathroom. But when I start the homeward sprint, the leg cramps hit, and I'm staggering and hobbling down the street, lurching from lamppost to lamppost, dragging my stupid dog, trying not to soil myself, and wondering if the neighbors think I've turned into a hopeless drunk.

Thanks to the misinformation you repeatedly provided, I've spent months pointlessly badgering my Esteemed Italian Lady Doctor to help me get reimbursement for the hundreds of dollars I've spent on Entocort. Thanks to the misinformation you provided, I've alienated my entire oncology team trying to get them to navigate your hellish website to find a solution.

Meanwhile, thanks to the exorbitant price of the Entocort, I am reduced to economizing by fishing capsules out of the sink when I vomit them up so that I can carefully rinse them off and keep trying to swallow them until I can keep them down. Unfortunately, I cannot economize by lowering the dose or going without the Entocort, as I would literally shit myself to death without it.

In conclusion, T—, I would dearly love to see the sad motherfucker whose symptoms are so much worse than mine that they are "funded for the requested indication."

Sincerely, etc.

TO: F—, Condominium Board of Directors

Dear F—,

As you know, I recently scanned the 100-page fire plan as a favor to the Board, because you needed a scanned copy to send to our insurance company. When some of the pages ended up upside down, you sent me an email asking if I intended for those pages to be upside down, and whether I recommended sending upside-down pages to the insurance company. It did not occur to me that you were being sarcastic. Indeed, I thought you might have said something like, “Oh, Ellen, thank you so much for scanning all the pages! Some of the pages are upside down, but no worries, we’ll fix that! Have a nice day!” Thus, in my ignorance, I sent back an email explaining how to turn the pages right-side up. But then you wrote back and ridiculed me for not understanding that you were being sarcastic. This hurt my feelings. I don’t understand why you have so much antipathy toward me. I’ve spent hours helping you when you had to deal with Periodic Information Certificates or Requests for Records, printing out the forms and even filling them out for you because you said you didn’t understand how to do it. Your emails flip between pleas for help and passive-aggressive tirades accusing me and other former Board members of incompetence and corruption. Maybe you are mad because we all resigned and you had to serve on the Board yourselves. But we resigned because you kept attacking us for being corrupt and incompetent! I think this building is cursed. I mean, seriously. It was built by a Theosophist architect, Joseph Hunt Stanford, in 1912, and named “Audley Court” after a very weird poem by Tennyson, also a follower of Theosophy, which was invented by an eccentric Russian émigré Helena Petrovna Blavatsky.

Suffice to say that even the nutters at the London Society for Psychical Research regarded Blavatsky not only as "a mere vulgar adventuress," but as "one of the most accomplished, ingenious and interesting impostors in history." Then, five decades later, in the Swinging Sixties, Audley Court was taken over by another "cult," so deemed by the *Toronto Star*, a group called Therafields led by another preposterous madame, Lea Hindley-Smith, who ended up owning dozens of properties in the Annex which she used for lucrative group therapy sessions based on her "lay psychoanalytical" approach, which she fabricated with no formal training or certification by any respected psychoanalytical body. I don't know. Maybe it wasn't the Theosophists and Therafields disciples who poisoned the energy at Audley Court. Maybe someone was murdered here and their ghost is haunting those of us stupid enough to buy into a small, self-managed condo in the Annex. Except it's not a very smart ghost; it's a banal, unimaginative piece-of-shit ghost. I honestly wonder if this fucking condo gave me cancer.

Sincerely, etc.

In the end, I do not send any of these letters. The act of writing them was supposed to exorcise my fears and frustrations.

It has not.

The anger remains, unabated.

And it's exhausting.

2024

8
Failure

As my increasingly unveiled anger takes over my mood and energy and life, I come to a realization that is kinda big: It's not just about the cancer. I'm not angry about having cancer per se. These things happen. What I can't deny is that I've been angry about a lot of things for a long time.

I don't feel compelled to analyze this. Seeing it and dealing with it is my task now. The last therapist I went to, Sheila, used to say that anger is a message to yourself. The message to me now seems to be: "You are an asshole."

Thinking about, and admitting to, my anger sends me into an unhinged tailspin of fuming rage and regrets. When I'm not writing angry letters, or glaring at people who won't get out of my way on the sidewalk, or wanting to kill anyone who comes near me at Shoppers Drug Mart, I'm obsessing about all the terrible things I've said and done in my life. I wonder why anyone is friends with me. Do other people feel this way? Are they pretending? Why would they go to the trouble? Maybe all the people around me don't really exist and my whole life is a matrix designed by my old buddy, Vengeful God, to torture me—he has surrounded me with imaginary "friends" who are wondering why I'm still waltzing around with an ECOG score of one, which is an oncology scale that means I'm fully functional and able to live independently and which I keep calling EGOT as a joke because that's the kind of pathetic humor I find funny these days. I hate myself. Am I fake, too? Everyone must think I'm a massive malingerer. They're looking at me like Elaine Benes watching *The English Patient*, thinking: *Die! Just die already!* They resent having brought me food and flowers because they think I've extorted their gifts and pity under false pretenses. I am the Old Buffoon in *The Brothers Karamazov*. *Am I lying? I don't know! I don't mean to lie!* I mean, I do lie. I fudge details about my illness—*treatments are going great! I'm great!*—to fend off serious questions. Or I preempt intrusive interrogation by bringing up the topic myself. Then I talk incessantly about my treatments, trying to make them sound interesting so people will feel they're getting a good return on their food and flowers. Eventually, as I concoct different versions, I forget whom I've told what.

It doesn't matter. I'm the one holding the cancer conch and I'm bloody well gonna use it. I make up narratives to suit the occasion or the audience or whatever current symptoms I have on display: dizziness, weight loss, arms covered in bruises and blown veins, bleeding fingertips, which is my atypical, split-skin inflammatory reaction to immunotherapy. I talk and talk and repeat myself. Endlessly. I swear a lot. Dog Park Peter asks if one of my side effects is Tourette's syndrome. I'm waiting for someone to put a pillow over my face to shut me up, for all our sakes.

Then there's my solitude. People worry about me because I live alone. In Winnipeg, I'd tell my brother when I took Sally for a walk down on the riverbank, invisible from the park fifteen feet above me. He'd keep an eye on my location in case the flashing dot suddenly stopped moving for any length of time, or conversely, started moving very fast in the direction of the twirling ice floes during spring thaw. Not that he'd be able to do much about it. But it felt good to know someone was watching.

In Toronto, my daughter is in daily contact, but as a touring musician, she's often out of town. Meanwhile, my friends keep an eye on me. Cathrin, who lives down the street, calls every day just to chat, but I eventually realize she's checking up on me, making sure I'm still here, able to answer the phone. When I have a sudden attack of whatever and need to go to ER, I call Johanna across the street, and while I'm still on the phone—it's like a sitcom routine: "Hello? Are you there?" *Ding-dong*!—she's here, hair askew, wearing what looks like pajamas, ready to drive me to the ER.

But the fact remains that I don't have a partner to find my body if I collapse in the night, or daytime for that matter. I'm pitiful because I don't have anyone to pick up prescriptions, or bring me ice water and a hot water bottle, to take me to ER when side effects get out of hand, to rub Voltaren on my back when the abdominal pain seeps through to my spine, to take out the garbage down the dangerously steep, not-to-code stairs at the back of my stupid condo. So yes, besides being a failure at fending off cancer, and failing to die from cancer in a timely manner, I'm also a failure at relationships.

I can never forget this because I am visited every sleepless night by my Grand Inquisitor.

How did you end up alone?

Okay, what if I was married? What if I had a perfectly nice husband, with thinning white hair, in a plaid flannel shirt and khaki Bermudas, sitting in his favorite chair, surrounded by newspapers on his lap, on the floor, on the table beside him, soaking up his spilled tea. We have a perfectly nice relationship. I ask him to apply Voltaren to my back and he gets up with a groan over his arthritic knees, and willingly complies. But he's not good at it. He's good at sex. We've never had a problem there. But here, I sense his faint repugnance at this form of physical contact. Instead of slowly rubbing the Voltaren into my sore back with a flat, warm hand, he pokes little gobs of cold gel onto my scrawny ribs with hard, curled fingers. It actually hurts. I ask him to stop, saying I suddenly remembered I need prescriptions picked up from Shoppers.

He says he'll go in a minute, and then he gets distracted. An hour later, I find him napping in the living room, so I put on my coat and runners and head out by myself.

I don't mind. I want to get out of the house. The walk will do me good. When I get home, he's awake: "Where were you, why didn't you wake me up, you didn't have to pick up your meds, I would've done it . . ." He wants to accuse me of going to Shoppers myself in order to make him look bad. It's a familiar pattern in our marriage, the way he looks for ways to portray me as passive-aggressive. His customary greeting on all occasions is, "Sorry I'm late! Don't kill me!" But I don't care: Therapy and age have taught me to ignore other people's lateness. It's a dead end; it's their problem; I always have a good book to read on my phone. "Oh God, I forgot to get milk. You're mad! I can tell you're mad!" I'm not mad. I already bought milk when I picked up my own prescriptions. "I'm going out. Will you be okay? I can stay home if you want." This is my cue to reassure him ten times that it's okay for him to go out, so he can feel like it's my idea, like it's me forcing him to go out. He always does whatever he wants anyway—he squanders hours of our lives with these stupid, defensive, repetitive arguments. He doesn't mind getting compliments from our friends about what a saint he is to take such good care of me. And he is! But deep down he resents it, which I understand and sympathize with. The problem is, he won't acknowledge it. Instead, his resentment comes out in snide remarks, or pretending not to hear me when he's in the kitchen and I call him from the bedroom, or taking a nap instead of picking up my prescriptions.

This pattern of his, this lack of self-awareness, makes me think uncharitable thoughts. He's not very smart. Why am I with this not-very-smart person? I don't want to take care of his feelings. I'm tired. I have cancer. Honestly, dear lord, it would be easier to live alone.

Why would you imagine such a negative scenario?

Because I'm an immature, resentful loser, I'm a terrible person. I don't deserve love. I don't know what love is. My relationships are transactional, competitive, and based in a power struggle that I will do anything to win. I distance people so I don't have to deal with intimacy. I'm a coward. I don't know how to argue without blowing everything up and walking out.

Lots of people are manipulative and shallow and morally weak like you. Yet they're still able to maintain long-term, committed relationships.

Because they know something I don't know! Because everyone has learned the trick of finding and keeping a mate and they're keeping that knowledge a secret from me. Because my Vengeful God wants to keep me alone and hopeless in the dark.

Why did you pick unsuitable men?

In my twenties I was obsessed with a shambolic Australian dilettante I'd met backpacking in Europe and had a back-and-forth relationship with him while he lived in England and I lived in France, and then we had occasional, chaste overseas visits with each other over the following decades, in Hamburg or Brisbane or Toronto after he got married to lovely Ursula, aka Ulla, a welcome delight in my life. I also settled down, and supposedly became engaged to a funny, smart, talented, successful graphic designer—except he broke off the engagement when I moved in with him. I ignored the red flag and moved in anyway—the clock was ticking and I really wanted a baby. I got my baby. Then, after nine years of both of us making a hash of that common-law marriage, I blew it all up and walked out.

I segued from frying pan to fire, taking up with a writer/actor/director in the middle of a midlife crisis. I was now in my early forties and having my own midlife crisis. I spent half a decade trying to rehabilitate the writer/actor/director who, in all fairness, was also trying to reshape me into the kind of partner he wanted. Then I blew it all up and walked out. That was twenty years ago. I've had other relationships since, none that stuck, obviously, because I'm a loser who doesn't know how to have an adult relationship.

I think we might have exhausted this examination into your failure at male-female relationships.

I'm also a failure at work. Everyone is laughing at me and my pathetic career. Everyone is more successful than me. I've never achieved anything. I make myself ridiculous talking about how I've worked on this or that TV show in a bid to validate myself as a real writer, to impress people. But nobody's impressed. They know I'm full of shit. They despise me. They should despise me! I'm tired. I don't want to lie awake thinking these thoughts. I don't know how to escape them. I'm stuck in the horse latitudes. Mute nostril agony.

Maybe I do need help.

9

Help

I join a support group that is both annoying and heartbreaking. There are eight of us. Two of the women are fantastic—smart and interesting, and who possess the rare talent of knowing how to behave in a group session. Two others are nice enough, but they do not know how to act in a group session. They talk over everyone else in a stream of consciousness that may or may not be about their cancer. The other three are younger women who I want to go take care of—they're so raw and vulnerable and in need of someone like me to go to their appointments with them and help them ask questions.

As for me, I'm the sixty-something lady who quietly listens for most of each session, then erupts halfway through when the two oblivious, talkative women are once more hijacking the entire exercise with their inane monologuing while the facilitator sits daydreaming in a corner of the Zoom grid.

After waiting in vain for the facilitator to say something—anything!—I weigh in: "Hey, we haven't heard how H's surgery went last week, if she wants to talk about it," or, "I'd love to hear how B's doctor appointment went, if she wants to talk about it." And guess what. H. and B. do want to talk about it! The facilitator, instead of finding me obtrusive, marvels at my input: "Omigod, Ellen, you're doing my job for me." Yes! Exactly!

But I can't hold back when one of the younger women says something like: "I don't know what stage my cancer is, and I don't like to ask my doctors, because they don't know." I tell her firmly: "Your doctors most certainly *do* know what stage cancer you have, and they absolutely won't mind if you ask them."

At other times, I'm rendered speechless, like when one of the talkative women says her grown children and husband are mad at her because she doesn't do their laundry anymore, and also they won't help her bring in the groceries from the car, and the facilitator says, "They're probably just scared." I want to shake the facilitator and tell the woman: *You need to sit your family down and tell them you understand they're scared, but you're scared too! And you need them to do the laundry and do the grocery shopping and suck it up and pull their weight!*

So the support group sessions weren't exactly a huge success in making me more Zen. When I relay some of this to one of the nurses I see every week at PMH, she says I should talk to someone in Psych Social. She'll arrange it. In due course,

I get a call from a woman who talks to me about resources that might help me deal with what I'm going through—websites like wellspring.ca, for example. She asks if I've received the packet that PMH provides for every cancer patient—a stack of booklets and a big, thick notebook with the title *My Cancer Journey*. I did receive it and threw it straight into the recycling bin.

Then she offers me general advice about how to cope. "Some people learn to live in the moment," she says.

I know where this is going and I start to physically cringe. *Oh, Vengeful God,* I pray, *oh please, please do not let her say it.* But my God forsakes me as per usual, and the Psych Social woman goes on to say: "Sometimes it's good to stop and smell the roses."

I wonder if there's a department at PMH that I can call to report her for inflicting trite hogwash on a stage-four cancer patient.

I'm about to thank her and hang up when she starts talking about a study I might be interested in. It's called CALM, their acronym for Managing Cancer and Living Meaningfully. "It's for people who are dying and facing existential questions," she says.

Yes, I am interested. I don't want to talk about cancer or dying, but I'm always interested in existential questions. And I know from experience that I can use therapy sessions to talk about my writing—it's basically a free focus group with an educated person who has to listen to you, no matter what you want to talk about.

Dr. H., a palliative care psychiatrist at Princess Margaret and assistant professor in psychiatry at the University of Toronto, is a young woman with a ready, radiant smile. She listens to my ideas for screenplays and my attempt to novelize a TV series (woman in crisis, solving a murder, her personal demons, etc.) for which I've outlined the entire long, twisty, thriller story, but which went nowhere because the network decided the main character—patently based on me—was too "unlikeable." I don't talk about cancer or any other issues. I want to use these sessions to have pleasant discussions about narrative structure and the meaning of life in general.

But Dr. H. is not fooled. Within two sessions, she observes that "shame and self-recrimination seem to come up a lot, thematically."

I feel exposed, but also relieved. I stop bullshitting and talk about other issues—like despite my fiancé David's assertion that there's not a goddamn thing I could have done about getting cancer I still feel guilt and shame around getting sick. I imagine my enemies whispering, *Ellen got this because she deserved it, with her reckless, job-quitting, peripatetic, party-smoking, binge-drinking, promiscuous ways.*

I think about the foolish risks I took as a young woman, backpacking alone in Europe, fending off predatory men as a matter of course. Like the family friend who, at the beginning of my Grand Tour, put me up for a night at his home in Sussex and, after a nice dinner, took off his clothes and chased me around the house—in and out of rooms, around the kitchen table, up and down hallways. It was like something from *Benny Hill*. Or the time I missed the ferry in Calais and asked for the time of the next ferry from the stationmaster, who led me into a dark office and started to grope me. I pushed him away, apologetically (in case he got angry), and awkwardly tried to hide behind a carousel of pamphlets, until people started showing up outside the glassed-in office and he let me go.

Another time, I was hitchhiking in Spain with another girl, Karen from Quesnel, B.C., when a man with a small boy in the front seat picked us up. What could be safer than a family man, right? Except then he took a side road, stopped the car, came around to my door, and opened it. I don't know what he was expecting—is this how Spanish men teach their boys about sex, or rather, sexual assault? I opened my Swiss Army knife and brandished it at him. He slammed the car door and drove us back to the highway. Karen and I got picked up by a tiny, very old man driving a giant semi. We both fell asleep, me in the passenger seat, Karen in the sleeping berth behind the front cab. I woke up in the dark to find myself completely alone. Then I heard the grunting and groaning of our tiny driver, followed by a stream of obscenities from Karen as she woke up to find the driver on top of her. She threw him off, and we grabbed our things and jumped out of the truck onto the empty highway—laughing our heads off. We mostly laughed about these encounters.

The only one that still gives me the creeps is when I was alone in Rome on a Sunday morning. I'd left my hostel to visit the Colosseum and the city felt magical—sharp sunlight piercing through morning mist, me feeling so happy and proud of myself to be taking in yet another incredible European city. As I got closer to the Colosseum, I saw two men, one in his twenties, the other at least sixty, approaching me and I readied myself to smile and step around them. But then the older one reached out and grabbed my crotch. I was shocked, helpless, humiliated. To this day, I can see his face, his glittering entitlement, satisfaction, hatefulness.

Not that it was any better in Canada. At university in Winnipeg, I dealt with predatory coaches, professors, and one frighteningly violent date-rapist, though we didn't have a term for it back then. We blamed ourselves for being gullible, or drunk, or too afraid to say no. Now, looking back, all the anger I should have felt then comes to the fore. Maybe I will feel less angry if I turn it into a joke. Like: There are an endless number of interview questions and questionnaires when you're being treated for cancer. They ask about your smoking and drinking history, presumably seeking to find correlations with possible causes of cancer. But maybe they should also ask questions like: *How many times have you been pawed, groped, molested, publicly humiliated, or threatened with violence if you didn't put out? How many times have you swallowed your anger because it wasn't appropriate or feminine or attractive?*

The trouble with making jokes with psychiatrists is that they don't laugh. They see through you and push you to do the difficult and painful work of unpacking what you're really talking about. I find I'm ready to do this. I have limited time left and I don't want to waste one second of it playing games with a psychiatrist like Dr. H., who is clearly smarter than me. And so, I drop the cool customer approach and let myself cry when we talk about unresolved family relationships. A big one is my long-standing tension with my two elder sisters. I'm angry with them for reasons I don't fully understand. I also feel guilty in case the tension between us is all my fault.

And, for the first time since I split from my partner thirty years ago, I talk about the guilt and shame I still felt about breaking up our family, destroying my daughter's life and my shameful exit in taking up with another man who was also scandalously leaving his family.

I'd had minimal contact with both sisters since leaving Winnipeg but now was able to call and chat with them both. As with other "huge relationship traumas" in my life, the result was anticlimactic. They were happy to hear from me; they hadn't really noticed that I'd "culled" them from my life. Maybe they were relieved I wasn't on their case all the time. Whatever. I accepted the new reality—I was lucky to have two admittedly eccentric, stoically Vanstoney but loving sisters who'd do anything for me, just like I'd do anything for them.

As for the shame and guilt around my family breakup, Dr. H. put it into perspective. Would it have been better if I stayed? Probably not. Did everyone survive? Yes, and we are all on good terms with one another. Do I need to feel guilty and ashamed around all the people I scandalized? Guess what. Other people are not thinking about me!

None of this happens overnight. And I have in no way addressed any issues stirred up by a stage-four cancer diagnosis. But maybe I'm on the right track.

2025

10
Collapse 1

In February 2025, I'm on the MK-0472 study. It's going well as far as I'm concerned—easy injections and no side effects. But no impact on disease progression either, it seems.

I learn this when I go in for my next dose and get a message from the trial nurse Kylie telling me to come to an examination room on the third floor instead of checking into the systemic treatment unit on the fourth floor. In the examination room, Kylie does my vitals and reviews all my symptoms and side effects. I'm feeling pretty good. Fatigue as per usual, but manageable. Pain that is mostly controlled by drugs. No vomiting.

Then Kylie tells me she has canceled my MK-0472 injection and that Dr. S. wants to talk to me. A few minutes later, my Beloved Italian Lady Doctor enters the room and pulls a chair over to sit close to me. She always sits close to me when she has bad news.

"The trial is not working," she says.

Okay. Does that mean I should prepare for another screening process to qualify for the next trial?

No. Dr. S. says she has no more trial options to offer me. Not only am I too atypical, but I'm now also too polluted. With all the drug trials I've been on, the potentially lingering effects of various products in my system make me a bad candidate for a new drug trial. Dr. S. explains that she'll definitely keep looking for another trial for me, but that it probably won't happen, and I realize this lab monkey is being decommissioned. Better than being terminated, I guess. But still a shock.

It's so strange. My beloved Dr. S., the most important person in my life over the past two years, is breaking up with me. She tells me I'm being relegated into the care of a palliative team whose job it is to make me as comfortable as possible while my disease progresses, and to prepare me for end-of-life options—a hospice if I want to die in a facility with twenty-four-hour staff. Or home care, if I want doctors and nurses to visit me as needed up to the end. MAID—Canada's Medical Assistance in Dying program—is also a possibility. I can't imagine pursuing it at this point, but I'm glad it is an option if things become unbearable.

After Dr. S. leaves the room, I rush to the sink to vomit.

I don't stop vomiting for the next two weeks. I can't drink or eat anything. I lose more weight. When I go in for a routine gynecology appointment, the doctor is so alarmed by my bloodwork that she sends me to urgent care for a blood transfusion. Soon after I'm hooked up and relaxing in my pod, my palliative doctor visits me. He tells me he's going to adjust my meds, doubling dosages of my various painkillers, adding an extra steroid for inflammation, and prescribing methylphenidate for energy. He tells me I only have a few months. "Like, six?" I ask him. He shakes his head. "At the outside."

It so happens that my friend Cathrin is with me, which is unusual, but I was only supposed to have a quick gynecology checkup after which we'd go shopping. Except now here we were, me whispering with the palliative doctor, her on the other side of my giant recliner, poking away at her phone. The low voice of the palliative doctor is barely coherent over the sound of the pump pushing the goopy blood from a stranger into my arm. I find this particular procedure revolting. I can't even look at the sticky bag of blood hooked onto the pole above my head. I trust that Cathrin can't hear anything, but even if she does, I know I can rely on her to pretend otherwise. Just like I pretend everything is fine after the palliative doctor leaves. She continues to busy herself with emails and her own calls while I phone my accountant for advice on how to transfer all my savings to my daughter with the least amount of tax burden. I call a lawyer about dissolving my corporation and another lawyer about putting my daughter's name on my condo title. I leave a message with a social worker about getting first dibs on a bed at the Kensington Hospice at College and Brunswick when I need somewhere to die. I ponder splurging on shopping, gifts, charitable donations, more TV subscriptions, with one small worry: What if he's wrong, and I spend all my savings and wrap up my affairs, only to find out I'm going to live longer and I need that money after all? It would be like Queen Latifah in *Last Holiday* (based on an old British film by J. B. Priestley), where she's told she has a rare brain condition and only weeks to live, so she quits her job, withdraws all her savings, and goes on a luxury holiday to Europe—only to find out the diagnosis was a mistake! I decide not to worry. Whatever happens, I probably won't end up on the street.

Once Cathrin and I are both off our phones, we get down to work on the most important task of all—planning a party.

11
The Party

It's Cathrin's idea that we host a joint birthday party because we're both turning seventy this year. Also, the last good party we were at was over a year ago, at Brown's. He and his wife Johanna throw excellent parties, with copious amounts of booze, signature cocktails, cannabis, and enough food to feed an army—Johanna comes from German stock in Pennsylvania, and no one will ever leave her house hungry. At that event, I mostly talked to people I talk to all the time. I was in a corner with my friend Don, whom I'd had lunch with the day before, when we were interrupted by Stephen, a shit-disturber who always asks me the same questions at these parties: "What's going on with your love life? Are you seeing anybody?" For some reason, in the past, I've always tried to give him a fun, entertaining answer. But then I go away afterward and resent it. So this time I countered: "Stephen," I said, "what is it about you married people that makes you feel entitled to ask single people about their sex lives? Like, what if I asked you about your sex life? Are you having regular sex with your wife? Is it any good? How often do you do it?"

God bless him, he had the decency to blush and splutter out an apology and start explaining that I reminded him of his favorite aunt, which was weird—why did he want to know about his favorite aunt's sex life?—but also felt like a sincere compliment. He went on to say that he met his wife at university and they'd been together ever since, which I took to mean that he hasn't had the kind of wild, adventurous sexual escapades he assumes I've had. The conversation was just getting real when we were interrupted by another friend who told us there was a celebrity academic at the party who was super rich and single. He had been married, someone else adds, but his first two wives died of cancer. "Oh, so I'm his type, then!" I quipped, but nobody laughed, probably because they couldn't hear me over the music.

In any case, it's high time somebody hosted another bash. For the rest of February, Cathrin and I talk daily about the food, the guest list, the wording and design of the invitation, the dress code (err on the side of fancy), and the time of day it should be (5 to 8 p.m.).

I don't know what I'd do without Cathrin. I met her thirty-odd years ago when she hired me to work at various magazines put out by *The Globe and Mail.* I subsequently followed her around as she moved from the *Globe* to *Maclean's,* the *Toronto*

Star, and elsewhere. Then she retired and turned herself into a successful writer: two books of memoirs, a *Star* column, and magazine features. Our respective writing schedules allow us to meet almost every day to toddle over to Summerhill Market or Shoppers or along Bloor to do errands. We have much in common: both from modest backgrounds, raised Catholic, with memories of wearing towels on our heads formed to look like wimples and veils that the nuns wore, and how we both wanted to be martyrs when we grew up. We wonder whether or not we'd have been Nazi sympathizers if raised in Germany during the War, or one of the bad nuns who mistreated children at residential schools. I fear I would've been a spineless follower of orders. She says no, we would've known it was wrong. Then she concedes that we might've been the kind of nuns who didn't join in, but who comforted the poor girls who were being tortured, which, she says, "would have been worse."

Our experiences diverge when Cathrin says the nuns at her school liked it when she challenged them. My nuns did not, and God help the child who embarrassed them when the parish priest came to class for a visit. We were encouraged to ask questions, supposedly, and I had one that had been weighing on me for some time: "If it's a sin to pray in a Protestant church, but then a murderer chases you into a Protestant church, is it still a sin to make a dying prayer to God to forgive your sins before the murderer kills you?" Before the priest had a chance to answer, Sister Rita blew her stack: "*Sit down!*" I was startled and embarrassed. I wasn't being sly. I was eight years old. It was a genuine question. To this day, I would like to know the answer.

One of our never-ending conversations is about writing—the mystery of unlocking a piece's structure; hating every word we type on bad days; reveling in fantasies about publishing a bestseller and/or Booker winner. We talk about writers who inspire us—Clare Keegan, Colm Tóibín, Martin Amis, George Saunders, Mavis Gallant—and wonder what their secret is. How do they make their writing crystal clear and easy breezy, dammit? We also talk about writers we hate, but who also inspire us because if their talentless crap can get published and become bestsellers, surely there's hope for us? Cathrin keeps offering to help with what I'm writing now—*Do you want me to introduce you to my agent? So do you want me to read what you have so far? How many words do you have? Do you have three chapters? You could send that out to a publisher and get a deal.* But I keep saying no. After years of pitching in print and then in television, I will never pitch anything ever again. I will write my memoir, and then my chosen publisher, Sutherland House, could take it or leave it.

In any case, the priority now is to pick the right date for the party. None of this is discussed out loud, but we both know it can't be too far out, given my dire but unmentionable prognosis. But it can't be right away because I'm still very sick and need time to recuperate and adjust to my new dosages and meds. In the weeks before the party, I experiment with dexamethasone, methylphenidate, hydromorphone, metoclopramide, olanzapine, pregabalin, budesonide, ondansetron, and Tylenol to find the right balance between unconsciousness, a manic jitteriness that the cocaine-like dexamethasone brings on, and pain-free bonhomie.

The party will be at Cathrin's house in case I'm incapacitated and suddenly can't host it *chez moi*. So even though we're hiring a bartender, and a caterer, and cleaners before and after, she still has a shitload to do: get her piano tuned, fix the light in her bathroom, which currently causes a small shock to anyone who uses the sink, move the furniture around, set up the kitchen and dining room for the caterer and bartender, and be home for flower deliveries.

On top of all this, Cathrin takes me shopping for an outfit, and when I worry that the shirt I bought is too big, but I'm too sick to go back to Andrews to try on another size, she takes the shirt back through a blizzard and picks up a smaller size. And then, when we both agree that the bigger size looks better after all, she travels through day two of the same blizzard to return the smaller one and bring back the bigger one.

We put my daughter Eliza in charge of the music. My friendship with Cathrin dictates my musical request: Carole King's *You've Got a Friend.* The plan is for Eliza's friend Ben to play cool, jazzy background music on the piano throughout the 5-to-8 p.m. party on the date we finally picked in early March, stopping only for speeches and for Eliza on her cello to play our chosen song, followed by *Happy Birthday.*

Two days before the party, Cathrin and I start freaking out. The truth is, neither of us has been able to hear or sing along to *You've Got a Friend* without bursting into tears every time. Is this what we want at the party? A lugubrious song about the sky above you growing dark and full of clouds while people hurt you and desert you and take your soul if you let them? Accompanied by heart-rending cello music? What is wrong with us?

But it's too late. When we express our concerns to Eliza, she firmly advises us that she and Ben have been rehearsing *You've Got a Friend* and that is the song they shall be performing.

The day before the party, I'm feeling okay. I get my hair done by Brigitte, a woman from the dog park who has a hair salon in her basement one street over. I explain to her that my raggedy bangs are a result of finding out I had a brain tumor a few weeks earlier. I was in the hospital and couldn't sleep, so I got up at 3 a.m. and used manicure scissors in the badly lit bathroom to give myself a haircut. Unfazed, Brigitte fixes the haircut, gives me highlights, and hot-irons her rescue project into a swingy sixties bob.

On the day of the party, I go to Cathrin's early and everything is perfect. Cathrin and I await our first guests. We've invited sixty-odd people and most of them RSVP'd yes, but you never know. At 5 p.m., a few people trickle in and we eagerly greet them and make sure they're properly introduced to each other and can find the bar. It's still nerve-wracking, but we're starting to relax. By 6 p.m., a mob of guests has descended—there's an actual lineup outside the front door—and we finally relax. Where to put their coats, where to get drinks, making introductions—there's too much noise and chaos to bother with the niceties. We wander off to enjoy the party and leave our guests to take care of themselves.

The only thing left to fret about is our speeches. Cathrin has hers printed out in large type on two sheets of paper. Mine is bullet-pointed on an index card in my pocket, but I don't need it after rehearsing my main points at home for two days: I stand up before the crowd and talk about how I knew this party would be a success because our guest list contained the best people in the world—a theme Cathrin picks up with her speech about friendship and what it means to her. Then she introduces Eliza and Ben.

I start to worry that I didn't thank Eliza more effusively in my speech. I'm a bad mother who's always been too reticent about her and her accomplishments. I'm trying to change, to be more openly proud of her. It's because I'm *too* proud! And I'm a Vanstone. I remember my mother coming home from a party once, miffed at another guest who apparently wouldn't shut up about her children. "You don't go out and talk about your children," my mother exclaimed. "Nobody wants to hear it!" I took it to heart. Now I look at my daughter, seated in front of me with her cello, her silken blonde hair gleaming in the lamplight, her long, slender fingers—she has beautiful hands—poised to begin, and I'm bursting with fearful pride at how lucky I am to have her. She's always been a mystery to me, especially since she hit puberty. I remember watching a video of Anne Frank's father saying that reading her diary was like both a "gift and a gut-punch." Don't get me wrong. Eliza and I have always had great talks about the meaning of life, about our relationships past and present with friends and lovers, and whether or not to get bangs. And I can thank cancer for giving me the chance to see how well she handles this crisis in our lives, and how I have been capable of woefully underestimating her—a revelation and definite gut punch when she points this out in one of our joint sessions with Dr. H. Calmly, clearly, she expresses her frustration with my failings, like how she wants to know my specific wants and needs instead of being sheltered like a child.

I look at her now, a woman suddenly taller than me, languid, thoughtful, fully in her element as a performer, ready to sing *You've Got a Friend* with utter confidence. She has a beautiful voice. And, just as we feared, the tears begin to flow. But they're good tears! People sing along—then laugh when Eliza tells them the next song will be happier, and launches into *Happy Birthday*.

The party goes late, which is fine. I hug my daughter every time I run into her in the swirling mix of partyers. I've calibrated my steroids and methylphenidate to make sure I stay awake past 8 p.m., and in fact, I last until past 10 p.m. People keep telling me how great I look, which I take to mean how not-near-death I look. I'll take it.

No one seems to mind that I'm still alive.

12
Plateau

By April, I start to feel better overall. My head clears, and I start to deal with my anger issues, such as (a) how angry I have been for so long; (b) how relieved I am to not feel so angry anymore; and (c) how my body feels different.

The last realization comes while I'm lying on my couch at home, and I notice how rigidly I'm holding the yoga position called Shavasana, or "corpse pose." It reminds me how many times over the past three years I've been asked to *hold still, don't breathe,* while I'm standing in front of an X-ray machine with my arms raised. Or lying on my side in a fetal position while something is injected into my spine ahead of an exploratory procedure. Or having my head bolted to the gurney for gamma-knife radiation to my brain. Or not daring to move a millimeter while giant needles are plunged into various organs for biopsies. And always, always holding my breath in case any tiny movement risks incurring inaccurate results or excruciating pain. Like the time a rookie doctor sank the biopsy needle into an area that wasn't anesthetized and it was so painful that I actually screamed. It was entirely his fault, and he was mortified, but the thought of that happening again made me even more vigilant about remaining deathly still for all my procedures. *Adopt corpse pose. Don't move. Don't breathe.*

Now my body is my own again. I'm allowed to move and breathe. I no longer need literally bracing anger to hold myself together.

All my life I've been skeptical about breathing exercises, mindfulness lessons, meditation, herbal tea—all those approaches that promise an ability to "let go" and "live in the moment" and even (barf) "smell the roses." Nothing has ever worked for me, it seems, except getting cancer.

I ask Dr. R., one of my palliative doctors, if she notices patients with advanced cancer changing their attitudes in any way.

"Yes!" she says. "We see it in patients all the time. We call it double awareness," which she goes on to explain means a new awareness of your mortality, which enables you to see things differently. Later, when I Google the term, I find an official definition: "The term 'double awareness' has been used in the context of advanced cancer to describe a person's capacity to be engaged in the world while preparing for impending death." The definition comes from a research study co-authored by my PMH psychiatrist Dr. H., which is good because now I can discuss it with her.

Over the months from fall 2024 to winter 2025, with Dr. H.'s help, I deal with my anger and grudges against various parties who have tried to destroy my life over the years. Like how I was the one who always phoned my sisters and they were never the ones who phoned me. So you'd think they'd notice when I came back to Toronto and stopped phoning them. Nope. Nothing. I writhed with worry about how hurt and bewildered they must be feeling at my silence. Was I being unfair? Would they punish me for it? But I stayed firm. If they wanted to reconcile with me, all they had to do was pick up the phone instead of taking it for granted that I would always call them. Eventually, a family matter necessitated a conversation with my sister Dianne. I was trepidatious. Would she answer the phone in tears? In a rage at me? Would she answer the phone at all?

She did answer and her first effusive, friendly words were, "Omigod, I haven't heard from you in ages! How are you?"

Jesus. This was so typical. I called my other sister, Valerie, and got the same reaction. My plan to destroy them both had failed! Maybe they liked it better when we had less contact? Whatever. I sank into the good feelings between us and let go of my grudges—I could hardly remember what they were. This double awareness business was like magic! When an old resentment did arise, I suddenly had the ability to stew on my own for a day or two, and then let it go. I accepted my role: I am the one who phones.

Unfortunately, the family matter that helped lead to more insight on my part was due to cancer, but not mine. Val was diagnosed with lung cancer just before Christmas in 2024 and died a few weeks later. My last phone conversations with her were tension-free and loving. Then, when I collapsed with my dire (but incorrect) prognosis soon after that, my sister Di immediately flew to Toronto. When not waiting on me hand and foot, she busied herself with cleaning my condo top to bottom and carrying out small repairs in the kitchen and bathroom. Most important, she wasn't the least bit squeamish about all my symptoms and nausea. She did, however, refuse to leave until I got rid of Sally.

I acquired Sally in 2021, when I was living in Winnipeg under perfect circumstances for pet ownership. My decrepit, squirrel-infested bungalow shack was immune to any more animal dirt and damage. I had time to walk a dog three times a day down by the river. So I went online, only to find that, thanks to all the other Covid clichés like me, you couldn't find a dog for love or money in 2021. One site for rescue dogs featured the same four sad cases month after month. The most viable candidate was an old, disabled, traumatized mutt who came with a list of warnings along the lines of "Do not adopt this dog if you have allergies, if you've never dealt with a rescue, if you have children, if you have furniture," and so forth. Then, a few weeks after I gave up, a woman in Portage la Prairie called back to say she had extra puppies. I could see online that she and her husband only bred dogs as a sideline to their orchard business. But the husband was a geneticist connected to the University of Saskatchewan, which also seemed like a good sign—his area was haskap berries, which are like fatter, hardier, sweeter blueberries, but he probably knew more than the average person about dog breeding as well.

In May 2021, Di and I drove the eighty-five kilometers to Portage la Prairie and picked up several jars of haskap berry jam, two pies, and my eight-week-old puppy, whom I named after Sally Wainwright, the writer/creator/showrunner behind the TV series *Scott and Bailey* and *Happy Valley*. Our first year in Winnipeg was idyllic—long walks down by the river and daily playdates with a border collie named Willow down the street. I learned that other dog owners can be a crapshoot. Many of them are weird, or weirdly aggressive, and the conversations are repetitious: *How old is your dog? What kind of dog is it? What kind of food do you buy? Where did you get your dog?* In one dog-park session, after everyone talked about how their mutts were all rescues, I told them: "I rescued Sally from a really expensive dog breeder in southern Manitoba." That shut them up. Maybe because they thought I was weird and aggressive.

Few of them ask you questions about yourself—that is, until I got to Toronto and met Dog Park Peter and his giant mongrel, Ursula. He and I got right into it. We met in Jean Sibelius Park between our two homes at 6:30 every morning, rain or shine, seven days a week, and bonded over childhood memories, politics, our children, music, and movies. When other dog owners started showing up, I resented them at first, but Peter delighted in hosting all comers. The king of Sibelius, he steamed past all the routine dog questions to interrogate people about themselves. Owning a dog in Toronto changed my life. I didn't grow up here, with friends in all kinds of different professions in adulthood. All my Toronto friends I know through work—mostly journalists like me who've never had "normal" jobs. Then, because my daughter went to schools outside the neighborhood, I seldom met nearby parents from various walks of life. The condo building I live in might also have been a problem. The man in the house to the south practically put his back out every day trying to avoid eye contact, because, I suspect, he thinks we're all renters, God forbid. Or maybe it's because my condo is cursed and he can smell the satanic stink all its inhabitants give off. In any case, thanks to Sally, I am now friends with people on surrounding streets whom I'd never have met otherwise. I feel connected to my neighborhood for the first time since moving to Toronto forty-six years ago. We invite each other to dinner parties. Peter is my dog park guardian, protecting me from our romping dogs, or walking me home when I'm looking the least bit shaky.

The friendships remain even after I lose Sally. I take my cue from Larry, who is also a dog owner, but never brings her to the park so early, "because she likes to sleep in." So he with his mug of coffee, and I, with my thermos of tea, join the group at dawn to enjoy the never-ending conversation with our neighbors. They all understand why I had to give up Sally. She was perfect for our first few months in Toronto, then suddenly turned into the worst dog of the bunch. Running out of the park onto the street. Chasing bicycles and little kids on scooters. Leaping the fence to poo in the soft, clean sands of the children's playground while parents screamed at me to control her. Peter blamed me—saying it all started with my sudden disappearances for hospital visits. The friends I relied on to take Sally were unbelievably generous—taking in Sally at the drop of a hat when I had to go to ER or stay in hospital for a few days. On one occasion, friends Janice and David blithely ignored my erratic behavior when I showed up at their house in the middle of the night because I was playing hooky from the hospital and wanted to take Sally home—only to have me wake them up again twenty minutes later after an irate doctor phoned and ordered me to get myself straight back to the hospital. I knew Sally was in good care wherever she was suddenly taken in, by my niece Ruth, or Ian and Sue. But Peter was right: my sudden disappearances affected her. The Covid-cliché relationship between us was pathologically co-dependent—to the point that when I had bouts of nausea, she also threw up within twelve hours.

On top of this, as my sister Dianne pointed out, even if Sally was good and calm, she was still a lot of work. I'd hired dog walkers seven days a week for the midday walk, but I still had to take her out for morning and night pees, and most days I was physically incapable. At a certain point, when she had her monthly attacks of diarrhea after eating garbage in the park or getting too many treats from other dog owners, I started to just let her out the back door of my condo and let her do her thing wherever. She'd race down the back steps into Bob and Donna's well-tended garden and blast away into their periwinkle. If I was feeling well enough, I'd put on boots and a coat over my nightie and go down to redirect her into the rental property to the west (who cares about renters, right?), where it was easier to find and pick up her droppings. But after a while, I didn't bother. Hopefully, some kind of winter-proof bugs would eat it all up before spring came.

Miraculously, my friend Nora was visiting one day when Dianne was still here and volunteered to foster Sally until she could find her a new home. I was so sick at the time that I merely acquiesced and left Di and Nora to work out the details. Now, months later, I still can't believe how lucky I am. Nora already had two rescue poodles of her own, so she knew what she was in for. But it was a lot. Besides making sure Sally got fed, walked, and groomed on a regular basis, Nora also spent hours vetting prospective new owners who came to us through word of mouth. She consulted with me at every step, but I trusted her to make the final decision. We had three or four potential owners, but either they fell through (one couple's surrogate mother had just got pregnant) or Nora didn't trust the vibe of this or that applicant.

Finally, a couple contacted us via a mutual friend. They had big rolling properties in Aurora, Georgian Bay, and Chester,

N.S. They'd had large dogs before. And they seemed to love Sally when they came to Nora's house for an interview. They took Sally for a trial weekend, then emailed to ask if she could stay a few more days while they checked her compatibility with a relative's labradoodle. Nora and I were ever so slightly miffed—they seemed to think they were interviewing Sally, while we thought they should've understood that they were the ones on trial. No matter. They decided to keep her and sent photos of her in her new home. I liked the way the husband sat with her on the couch, his hand firmly on her haunch to give good scratches. I thought I'd never recover after Sally left. At the same time, I was grateful every day I didn't have to take her out for a walk, or go lift a twelve-kilogram bag of dog food into my car, then carry it up the stairs into my condo, or try to lift my seventy-five-kilo mutt into the bathtub when she came home covered in mud.

I still don't know what I would've done if Nora hadn't stepped in. If I believed in God, and if the Catholic Church were run by women as it should be, I'd nominate her for sainthood.

13
Collapse 2

It's June. I am doing great. I've joined the Jewish Community Centre and am taking pickleball lessons and going to Tai Chi. I've signed up for pottery classes at the Gardiner Museum with Cathrin. I buy Nike court runners and New Balance walking runners and a bunch of new t-shirts for all my sports and pottery-throwing activities.

Then, one morning, I wake up and can hardly breathe. Something is pressing against my lungs and my abdomen is distended and sore. I go to the ER at Toronto General and wait for three hours. But the wait time on the board says there's another eight hours to go, so I give up and go home, where I can at least lie down and take the pressure off my lungs. I phone my palliative doctor, who sends me for a CT scan two days later, on Friday. On Sunday, I get a call telling me to show up in the Radiation department at Princess Margaret the next morning. There, they do another CT scan in order to mark the target area, and the next day, I come back for a massive dose of radiation on my liver, spleen, and stomach.

I've had radiation before—on my groin and my stomach—and it was no big deal, so I'm not expecting any side effects. I expect to bounce back and resume my life of cancer-oblivious socializing with a few extra naps thrown in. I am mistaken. About five minutes after the treatment, as I walk upstairs to the lobby, I start to double over with pain and nausea. I manage to call an Uber, which arrives quickly. I clumsily get in, then start retching into my purse. The driver rolls down all the windows, anxiously asking me, "Are you all right?" Don't worry, I tell him. "I have nothing to retch up, it's just dry heaving."

I survive, but this time I don't bounce back. I'm always tired due to low hemoglobin and the persistent anemia most cancer patients get, but the fatigue I feel after that dose of radiation is different. I feel as if I've been run over by one of those big asphalt-roller trucks that flatten characters like Daffy Duck. Unrelenting nausea kills my appetite. I watch the scales go down each day: 106 pounds, 103, 102, 101, 98. The thing about being underweight is that it makes you feel weak, physically and psychologically. When I touch the teapot by mistake and it burns my finger, I start apologizing. To the teapot. I'm a ghost, a transparent grey entity, struggling to be seen and heard. The steroids I'm taking cause the skin on my arms and hands to bloom with angry red bruises at the slightest amount of pressure—brushing my hand against a cupboard door or kitchen drawer. I have bumpy little metastases on my torso, spine, and neck. I wear only collared shirts and dresses in order to hide them. I have an entire wardrobe of clothing I can no longer use because I don't want to expose my bony arms, bruises, and metastases to the world.

The palliative doctor tells me my peritoneum is thickening, which will cause problems with my digestive system, and my kidney is swelling due to a blockage caused by a tumor on the ureter, which they can totally fix—but won't, because I have so much galloping disease in my liver and elsewhere, there's no point in trying to play whack-a-mole with palliative surgery at this point. I could tell Eliza, or Cathrin, or any of my siblings about these developments. But the thought of the conversation depresses me. They would listen sympathetically. They would worry. But there's nothing they can do.

So much for all my fitness plans. I cancel my membership at the JCC and give away my runners (which unbeknownst to me are actually kind of "cool") to my daughter. I go with Cathrin to the first few pottery classes but we're terrible at it and we both hate it. The only reason we keep going is that it costs so much, and we're too competitive with each other to quit.

I become depressed. Where's double awareness when you need it? I try to listen to music but my old standards are no comfort. Like that girl Brandy, laying whisky down and wandering around town, because the man she loves, this man who always told the truth, Lord, he was an honest man, can't be with her because his life, love, and his lady is the sea. Which I think, okay, fine, but he's probably still fucking her when he sails into port, and what's she supposed to do if she gets pregnant? I wonder if Brandy knows that other girl who wanders around another town—Bitter Green, they call her—walking in the sun, loving everyone, waiting for her master, some sailor or prisoner who died somewhere in the mist dreaming of her kiss, but then one day, a weary stranger comes to town and visits the churchyard and kneels and lets his tears fall in the dust because he's too late. Why didn't he just write her a letter for God's sake? All this dumb male behavior is not relaxing.

I start to feel afraid. I'd had fleeting moments of fear after my initial diagnosis, but now it's increasingly present. I think about something a friend told me years ago. We were at a wrap party for a TV show, and I got very drunk, legless, on the verge of making a bad decision with the show's married, womanizing music composer. Thankfully, my friend Deng and her husband Peter, one of the show's producers, rescued me. The two of them half-carried me to their car and drove me home. At my door, just before they left, Deng patted me on the back and whispered in her Thai accent: *Remember. You're born alone. You die alone.* It might seem like an odd thing for her to have said, but it was exactly the right thing for me to hear at that moment. It gave me a kind of stern comfort that I've thought about often.

I bring this up with Dr. H. I tell her about my sudden, ongoing fear of dying, expecting her to give me tried-and-true tips on "How to dispel your cancer fears!" Instead, she advises me to go deeper into the feeling and sit in it. *What are your fears? What are you afraid of specifically?*

I make a list:

- Pain
- Loss of control over my daily activities and environment
- The indignity of my body giving out while people are watching, i.e., having an ugly, disgusting death instead of a painless, decorous Lifetime movie fade-out
- Wondering whom to invite if I choose MAID to end it all. Where do you draw the line with family and friends? Will people be mad if they're not invited?

I wake up in the middle of the night thinking: How pathetic. This is my brand—worrying about what other people will think while I'm on my literal deathbed.

I notice that none of my fears are about death itself—about what lies on the other side. Is this because it's too scary to think about? Or is it because my rational beliefs are true, i.e., there's nothing on the other side so there's nothing to be afraid of. I find the idea of nothingness relaxing. I hope there's no reincarnation—the thought of living another life sounds exhausting. Though I would accept a heaven where I'm allowed to dart down to Earth now and then to fix things I regret, or stand up to bullies I was too weak to confront.

I enjoy imagining my version of Heaven. There would be fluffy clouds and soft robes, but my Vengeful God is far away in a distant, boring, religious neighborhood of Heaven that he never leaves and I'll never visit. Little café tables dot the landscape, where I'll drink strong coffee with friends and relatives, and then, during another glorious evening sunset, kick back with my mom, smoking Export As, drinking wine and getting tipsy but never hungover, and asking her questions I wish I'd asked when she was alive. I'd play catch with my dad, who'd be fit and strong and would've forgotten the time on Earth when he was sick and scared before he died. Both my parents are good, fun, interesting people, and in Heaven they'll be their true selves without being distracted or beaten down by money worries, or raising six wild-minded kids in a too-small house, or being tortured at how incompatible they were—my chauvinist dad versus my feminist mom—while still loving each other too much to blow it all up and walk away.

I'm counting on what I've been told by my palliative doctors—that the end tends to come after a quickish physical decline, at which point people usually sleep a lot and are relatively comfortable because there's plenty of symptom relief on offer. This has been true throughout my illness. All my various doctors have prescribed as much hydromorphone as I want. Early on, when I asked one doctor if there was "any danger of long-term addiction" vis-à-vis all the opiates I was taking, she hesitated, then answered carefully, "Uh, I don't think that's anything you have to worry about."

So my plan is to be tired and sedated and still firmly in denial so I won't have to be brave. My daughter and relatives and close friends who surround me at my demise will not be treated to any smiling, peaceful, philosophical goodbyes. We're all going to pretend this is just another temporary side effect, and that I'll be up and about soon.

The fear abates somewhat, but I can't shake my depression.

There's one thing that keeps me going: I'm booked to take a massive dose of psilocybin in mid-July as part of yet another drug trial.

14
Psilocybin

The psilocybin session is part of a PMH study called PEARL: "Psilocybin-assisted Existential, Attachment and Relational Therapy for Patients with Advanced Cancer: A Phase II Open-Label Trial." I've spent weeks being screened, involving bloodwork, physical exams, endless questionnaires, and interviews, during which I try not to appear too cheerful, which would disqualify me, or too depressed, in case they think I'm suicidal, or too eager, in case they think I'm a drug addict.

After finally being accepted, I have a series of pre-dosing sessions with the two psychiatrists who will be with me during the six- to eight-hour dosing session. I'm relieved to hear that one of them will be my brilliant PMH psychiatrist, Dr. H. The other one, Dr. M., is a cheerful woman with whom I click instantly.

When Dr. H. first asked if I was interested, I instantly said yes, believing the drugs would at least offer a fun, psychedelic, distracting trip with possibly some flashbacks over the weeks following. I wasn't worried about a "bad trip." I've indulged in alcohol, cannabis, cocaine, LSD, and mushrooms in the past, with the latter being the only one that was pure fun with no hangover, fatigue, or depression afterward.

But after several prep sessions with Dr. H., I start to understand that the experience is less about getting high and more about aiming for a permanent, positive shift in attitude, or perception, or understanding, or all of the above. As Dr. H. explains it, the theory is that the drug can benefit stage-four cancer patients by opening them up to new ways of thinking, the same way that plain old psychotherapy can cause dramatic shifts in some people's point of view about themselves and the world around them. She says that a lot of people who've gone through the experience tend to have a feeling of being more connected to everything—people, the world around them. This makes sense, judging by the documentary *Fantastic Fungi* I saw years ago, and which left me with the impression that fungi are interconnected around the globe, basically holding the planet together like a giant, painstakingly crocheted support system.

Later, I check out the study online. According to the UHN website about PEARL, "the psilocybin induces an altered state of consciousness that is thought to increase emotional openness and empathy and enhance neuroplasticity—the brain's ability to reorganize neural connections."

Here's what I know about the session so far. I show up at Toronto General at 8:30 a.m. on the dosing day and proceed to a room on the seventh floor that I've already seen. It's been tarted up to resemble a luxury hotel suite—all white and beige furnishings and a big comfy bed. I will pick up prescriptions for several "rescue drugs"—anti-nausea, anti-psychotic, and blood pressure meds. The two psychiatrists who will be monitoring me throughout, Dr. H. and Dr. M., won't interact with me unless I initiate it. I have to give consent to be touched in case I need any literal hand-holding or back-patting during the session, or in case they have to restrain me from leaving. They want the experience to be interior, so I'll have an eye covering and headphones with music chosen by a musical therapist. The music is supposed to guide people through the experience. It's instrumental and hopefully unrecognizable, which makes sense. Familiar old songs could definitely lead to sad, bad thoughts if they trigger the wrong memories.

After the session, my daughter will pick me up, take me home, and spend the night. The next day I'll meet with Dr. H. and Dr. M. again for an "integration session" to talk about the experience and, presumably, help me process it in a way that provides maximum benefit.

I have high hopes for the whole exercise. I may be counting on it too much. I want it to make me happy and well-adjusted for the rest of my life. I'm also afraid it might go bad and I'll spend the whole day crying. It doesn't help that I've been watching *Nine Perfect Strangers*, with Nicole Kidman overdosing a bunch of messed-up clients with shrooms, then manipulating them throughout their intense trips.

When I discuss these fears in a final prep session with Dr. H., she tells me, "Whatever happens, it'll be something we can work with." This makes me feel immensely better. I like to be productive. I can take whatever comes.

I show up at 8:30 a.m. on the day wearing comfortable clothes—a linen shirt and loose pants. I've brought sheets and a duvet cover for the bed, the rescue medications, along with my own supply of hydromorphone and Tylenol, which I always carry in case of breakthrough pain.

The three of us have also brought things that are significant to us. Dr. M. has a stone from a certain location that was important in her life. Dr. H. has brought some lines from Rilke: *This more human love (endlessly considerate and light and good and clear, consummated by holding close and letting go) will resemble that love that we so arduously prepare—the love that consists of two solitudes that protect, border, and greet each other.*

I'd thought of bringing my mother's Bulova watch, which was still ticking if not accurately telling the time after sixty years or more, and a tie clip and cufflinks of my dad's. My memory of them both is uncomplicated and full of love. But then I thought that was looking back instead of forward. I'd been upset in recent sessions with Dr. H. when she asked me to talk about the future (*what future ffs?*). But a conversation with my niece Ruth, a clinical psychologist, the day before had helped. "The future is tomorrow," she'd said. "What do you want tomorrow?" She knew I was excited about the experience but had become increasingly anxious and fearful as the day approached. "Don't be afraid to be raw and open," she told me, echoing the advice Dr. H. had given me. "Sometimes that can lead to the best outcome."

And so, I tell Dr. H. and Dr. M., the item I've brought is about the future: the IVF petri dish that held the embryo which—through a miracle that still overwhelms me—became my daughter. Eliza represents the future for me, and my future will always be tied up with hers.

Dr. H. asks if I want to meditate before we start. I'm not a meditator, but agree—what harm could it do? We close our eyes and breathe together, slowly in, slowly out. Dr. H. does a body scan as we breathe, gently going from head to toe in a soothing, rhythmic voice, which makes me feel thoroughly relaxed.

Finally, Dr. H. takes out the psilocybin, has me read the label on the pill container to make sure I understand what I'm taking, and drops the pill into a stone bowl, and passes it to me. I take the pill. We sit and chat some more until I start to feel the effects of the drug. I go to bed and lie down, with my eyes covered and headphones firmly in place. Dr. H. adjusts the volume of the musical soundtrack, and I start to hallucinate.

I was expecting something wild, like the final scene in *2001: A Space Odyssey*, where astronaut David hurtles through space and time and spectacular visual phenomena to a final scene where he becomes a fetus. So I'm a bit disappointed when my hallucinations start off as unremarkable playing cards, albeit with intricate designs on the back that morph into swirling, intensely colorful patterns. Then I'm frightened when insects start emerging out of the patterns and coming toward me. They're intricately made of tiny jewels with red ruby eyes, and they're gorgeous, but I hate insects. I keep cringing away trying to avoid them, but they keep coming. At this point, I realize there are two Ellens—Dream Ellen fending off tiny attackers, and Lucid Ellen, who's watching the dream and thinking, *the hell with these bugs, I don't want to waste my whole trip being attacked by insects!* It seems to go on for hours. Eventually, a master bug appears, a big fat monster with clusters of loud whirring wings, malevolent red eyes, and a look of smiling triumph. I realize it's the Devil. After wiping him away over and over, I think *okay, enough already,* and I decide to let him come at me. He charges straight at my face. I close my eyes and brace for impact, but at the last second, he veers away. And that is the end of the insects.

This routine continues with other dreams.

Dream Ellen wallows in endless, anxiety-filled scenarios with characters I thought I'd dealt with in my life—problematic friends, my sisters—while Lucid Ellen is irked. I love my sisters! I've resolved my issues with them! I don't want to waste this trip rehashing old grudges! But eventually, I notice they're not looking at me. Val and Di throw me fond looks, then ignore me because they are busy with their own dreams.

I start to realize I have control over these dreams. This brings a feeling of confidence and I'm rewarded with a series of adventure dreams, the storybook kind that you never want to end. The one I remember best is me surrounded by handsome young pirates in a creaking ship on a turquoise sea flecked with whitecaps under a pink sunset sky. They are busy pursuing the usual business of piracy, taking over other ships and plundering them for treasure, but they are pacifist pirates who somehow conduct their business without violence or bloodshed.

I'm disappointed when the adventure dreams evaporate and I start having boring dreams about going into beautiful rooms or gardens where a bed is made up for me. Sometimes I lie on the bed, and then can't breathe. Thank God for the breathing exercise Dr. H. led me through that morning, which calms me down and allows me to take control of what's happening. Meanwhile, Lucid Ellen has deduced that these dreams are about dying. I'm acutely aware of the two psychiatrists observing me and wonder if this whole psilocybin trip is a trap to lure me into dying peacefully right there and then. But then I think: *It wouldn't be very good for Dr. H.'s PEARL results if all her study participants died during their sessions.* Lucid Ellen lets go of all these thoughts and decides to just let it happen.

And then, nothing happens. Or maybe I die and don't notice it; I just find myself in Heaven, which I now see is a prominent feature in all the death dreams—a kind of sidebar filled with fluffy clouds.

I want to keep dreaming, but I'm fully awake now and get up off the bed. I talk to Dr. H. and Dr. M. about the experience while they monitor my vitals and we wait for Eliza to arrive. I talk again with Dr. H. the next morning, which helps me remember more details about the experience. But otherwise, I don't want to discuss it with anyone. I don't want to harden the experience into a narrative that isn't finished yet—I need to think about what happened, and what effect it has on me.

A lot of my trip involved feeling victimized by tormenters—insects, the devil, other people—all of whom turned out to be harmless, a byproduct of old fears and grudges hanging around like sticky lint in the back of my brain. But they were so easy to dismiss! The confidence I'd felt in controlling my dreams stayed with me in the days and weeks after the experience.

I took notes afterward, but I tried to let details arise without any pressure from me overthinking it. I remember more and more, including a dream about some married friends. The husband is busy doing something but stops when his wife asks him to do something she could easily have done herself. I wondered why he didn't point this out to her, at which point Dream Ellen thinks: *Oh. It's because they love each other.* And for some reason, this makes Lucid Ellen start to cry.

I started to think about love.

15
Platonic Love

I'm still in touch with my best friend from grade one at Our Lady of Victory Parish School in Winnipeg. As with my "fiancé" David, Maria and I have always kept in touch, despite the fact that she ended up living in South Carolina and voting as a Republican. We didn't talk for a couple of years after she voted for Trump in 2016, then slowly resumed communications with no mention of politics after that. I don't know if she's still a Trumper, and won't ask.

Our lives couldn't be more different. After taking Pharmaceutical Sciences at university, she eventually ran a pharmaceutical ad agency in Manhattan with her copywriting husband Tom, servicing clients in the US and Europe. They made enough money to retire young and live a carefree life of golf, pickleball, and BBQs with friends—while I continued, quite happily, to scramble as a freelance writer. Yet we never run out of things to talk about. We email to recommend books or argue about books we've recommended. She's changed my mind more than once about certain books and authors, which is not something that comes easily to me. I don't think I would've survived the nuns at Our Lady of Victory without her. She's been through personal tragedy in her life, yet has never succumbed to bitterness or regrets. Unlike me, she remained Catholic and still goes to church, so maybe that's the key to her positive outlook. Or maybe it's just her nature.

Just before I had my psilocybin trip, she sent an unusual email, full of raw emotion, which is never how we've communicated. She talked about how *"we've been there for each other through all the stages of life" and how "you never once judged me. Not once! (Even though it probably would have been beneficial at certain points.)"* She finishes with a declaration: "*Hopefully, you don't interpret any of it as me asking for some kind of support from you. You just need to know that I LOVE LOVE LOVE you.*" A week later, she sends another email, recommending a book, *Broken Country* by Clare Leslie Hall. "It's a love story with a twist," Maria writes. "But, when I thought more about it, I think it is a book about love in general—the love we experience as parents/children, husbands/wives, siblings, and friends—and how love can be selfish, selfless, deserved and undeserved."

It's one of those weird coincidences in life, when the universe starts handing you material that accords with what you're thinking about, or working through, or strenuously trying to avoid. So Maria's comments about love stay with me as I process my psilocybin trip, and I think about how I've thought about love in the past. How I was embarrassed by it, or thought it was weak to express it, or even feel it. Or how I allowed my Grand Inquisitor to torment me about my failure to achieve "true love."

How did you end up alone?

I didn't end up alone. I made choices that led to being alone. I like being alone. Also, I'm not really alone. I'm surrounded by family and friends who check in on me every day. In fact, sometimes it's a bit much—like I'm being stalked by loving well-wishers.

Why did you pick unsuitable men?

Were they unsuitable? All the men I've had significant relationships with are still in my life. They are valued, devoted, loyal friends. The shambolic Australian remains a man on the move, spending time since his early retirement living in various homes in the UK, Europe, Japan, and Australia (to this day I have no idea what he did for a living, but it obviously worked out). Our most recent correspondence consisted of me bundling up all his old letters and sending them to his *appartement* in Marseillan, France. I had no reason to keep them since they're completely illegible—I had better eyesight in the 80s and 90s and was more motivated to decipher every scrawl for signs of his passion for me. In vain, as I recall. Now I want him to read them and report back to me what we talked about back when we were in our twenties and thirties.

The next one, the graphic designer, now lives outside Toronto, but gets in touch when he's in town. We have a good relationship that's still evolving, not just because we share a child, but because we still care about each other's welfare. He's someone I can rely on to be frank with me. Like the time we had lunch after our split and were comparing our experiences on eHarmony. He'd had eighty-seven responses within twenty-four hours of joining. "What!?" I said. "I've had three responses after two weeks of membership." He thought a moment, then said: "You seem like the kind of person who should be single." It hurt my feelings at the time, not because he was taking a shot or being unkind, but because his observation felt true. It still feels true. I feel more like myself when I'm alone.

Even the writer/director of my forties—K.F., the world's worst boyfriend—is still a friend. He was generous in many ways to me when we dated. He unfailingly praised my talent as a writer and pushed me to be a better one. We still worked together after we broke up, though it wasn't easy. On one of his shows, I had to leave the building one lunch hour and go sit in my car to sob in private over what a colossal mess of my life I'd made with him. With no Kleenex or napkins to use, I took off my runners and used my thick cotton socks to blow my nose and wipe my face. I put the damp socks back on and went back to work. But no matter what hostile relationship battles went on between us, I knew I could still phone him day or night, and he'd answer, "Where are you? Are you alright?"

And then there's my fiancé, David. Our initial phone calls, then weekly Zoom calls, started off being about my illness, but soon became about everything. He tells me about a guy in our neighborhood who was wonderful and funny and smart but who had a hard life and died young. "He had serious hots for you," David tells me. "He said you were the girl whose bicycle seat he'd most like to sniff." Nice. I tell him my memories of him at med school—e.g., how he told me a doctor's tie was the dirtiest thing in the world. Not to mention how sexist they all were—using mnemonics like Fat Gents Eat Daisy to remember fastigial, globose, emboliform, dentate, the four nuclei in the deep cerebellum. We talk about our parents, our siblings, our children, distant relatives with weird personalities and mysterious lives. We argue about politics, and about how he's unconsciously, unavoidably sexist as a privileged white male over sixty.

We talk about love and how we never used that word when we were younger, and how we use it now with each other. He says he's loved other people, "but you're the only one I've loved all my life." I tell him I've always loved him. I think about how we make these declarations now, so calmly and unbidden.

"Do you think it would have worked out if we got married?" he asks.

"I don't think so," I say.

He's miffed. "That was quick."

"Well, what do you think?"

"It would have been a bloodbath," he says.

After I point out that he answered just as quickly as I did, we discuss our reasons. He says he was a selfish, surly bastard back then. I say it never would've worked because I was so immature and desperate and depressed and defensive and self-destructive. "You wouldn't have had a chance."

"We'd probably still be emailing once a month or so," he says, and then concedes, "but no, we wouldn't have this."

I talk about the platonic love between us, and how, thanks to my cancer, I've been surprised and lucky to have discovered how intimate it can be. He shakes his head. "You're such a Pollyana. You should call your book *The Bright Side of Cancer.*"

I laugh. "Actually, I was thinking: *Ha-ha, I Have Cancer and You Don't, Losers!*"

I want to talk more about platonic love, but he deflects—he's always going off on tangents—and starts talking about Aristotle: "Didn't he say there were three types of love: *eros, agape, philia*? Which would ours be?"

I shake my head: "I don't care about Aristotle, or any other male 'expert' on the subject. I want to talk about us, and our feelings."

He says, as he has said to me often over the past three years, "Christ, I've never talked about this stuff with anybody." But he never shies away from any topic I bring up. As we discuss platonic love, he says, "I know you don't believe this, but I still find you incredibly attractive." David has always been a shameless flatterer, so I normally brush off his compliments. But today, emaciated, pale, bruised, I think: *maybe I will believe it*. I talk about our few romantic encounters over the years, when we both happened to be single and crossing paths in one city or another. "I wish we'd met up more often and had more sex."

He agrees. "We should have gotten married in Winnipeg when I was thirty and you were twenty-nine. I was working at Deer Lodge and making $1,800 a month—a fortune in those days! Then I would've followed you to Toronto so you could take journalism at Ryerson. We would've had a couple of kids." But then, he goes on, I'd have had to deal with his surly behavior. I ask him what he'd have to deal with in me. He hesitates and says carefully: "Your episodic moodiness." I find this interesting. I didn't realize my suicidal depression back then was evident to anybody.

As with all our discussions of what might have been, he ends with, "But if we'd gotten married back then, we wouldn't have our kids today." I agree. My solution is to posit that we're married in a parallel universe. I tell him we got married in our early twenties, and it was fun and good for a while. Then in our late thirties or early forties, he stepped out on me and had an affair. I found out and was devastated! But a part of me was also excited because now I had a free pass to play around. There follows a sordid and regrettable period where we both have sex with a series of people until we realize there's no one out there better than what we have in each other. So we get back together and go to couples counselling, which is interesting and funny because we bond over how dumb couples therapy is, and we make gentle fun of our elderly, frizzy-haired, earth-mother couples therapist. I accuse him of wanting to sleep with her, which irks him in a way that I find hilarious. But we end up getting a lot out of it. We forge the kind of ideal marriage we both want: true partners who have each other's back.

One afternoon, when he's visiting me in Toronto and it's unfortunately during one of my bad spells—or maybe fortunately, since he's a doctor, after all—he brings me a hot water bottle and more ice water, and then we get to talking and he falls asleep on the bed beside me. We end up spooning through several layers of sheets and a quilt. When we wake up, he complains, "It still pisses me off that we missed out on fifty-five years of this."

I know what he means. But I also know the love we have now might never have happened if we'd gotten married in our twenties, or if I hadn't got cancer. So I answer with conviction: "But we have each other now."

He pauses. I feel like he's going to argue. But then he nods. "Yes. Yes, we do."

16
Writing

So you wrote a book, eh, Smartie Pants?

Yes, I did, with no thanks to you, I might add.

Excuse me?

Actually, okay, yes. You have been useful.

How?

You challenged me. You forced me to think through my insecurities. You stopped me, I hope, from becoming too precious about writing this book.

Thank you. So now what?

Now I face the final chapter.

I don't want to die, but we all die. Who's to say it will be easier when I'm eighty or ninety? As I write about love and friendship, I think about all my devoted friends and family—Cathrin, Johanna, Nora, Janice, David, Sue, Ian, Morwyn, Tecca, Ken, Gillian, Ron, Ian, Art, Dianne, Jay, Mike, Lindsay, Eliza Ruth—constantly checking in on me, or just making me laugh when I do see them, and I realize I never had to choose between family in Winnipeg and friends in Toronto. They were all there for me, all the time, even without cancer.

I think about how lucky I've been in my choice of siblings. Our easy camaraderie. In Winnipeg whenever my brother Mike was going to Canadian Tire or the Peavey farm equipment store, he called me. I always went. I love Peavey. Among all the tools and farming equipment I wish I had a reason to buy, it also has women's clothing. Real clothes that mean business. Once on a trip in his giant beige pickup truck, we spied a guy in a wheelchair rumbling down Jubilee toward the cloverleaf of traffic and overhead train tracks and impassable pedestrian walkways in the snow. And we kinda laughed, like "good luck, dude." He dropped by my house later to get something he forgot and I asked him, "You went back to help him, didn't you?" Yep. He offered the guy a ride, but the man declined. So Michael gave him twenty bucks and made sure he was safe in his path through the quagmire of slush and snowbanks.

Or Lindsay, our man of mystery and the consummate gentleman. He's a talented writer who didn't choose that path, which I try not to wish he had. People make their own choices. Even people like my siblings—who should do what I tell them, you know, *for their own good!* He doesn't talk much, which makes me worry he's angry. Which sometimes is the case—he's not a huge fan of the Internet, or corporate conglomerates, or government bureaucracy. But on other occasions, like when he's a bit high, he's wryly funny, the life of the frigging party. He's slim, health-conscious, silver-haired, self-contained. I keep seeing men his age on the street and for a second think it's him. I joked with Ruth once that for all I knew he was one of those men, actually living in Toronto with an entire separate family. "Honestly?" said Ruth. "That wouldn't surprise me one bit."

On September 16 of this year, I had a chat with my brother Jay. On September 17, he called to say he was on the next flight to Toronto, which was okay, but abrupt. He arrived in the nick of time. The day he landed, I fell twice, once face forward going down the stairs from my apartment to the outside world, then backward again at the café where I was meeting Nora. I fell backward as we were leaving. My head bounced off the concrete floor. People ran over to help. They wanted to call an ambulance. I just wanted to get home. I had a goose egg on my head for a few days but no concussion. Nora took my arm and helped me navigate the garbage and recycling bins that block our Annex sidewalks on Tuesdays. That was the last time I saw the outside world except from my balcony. Meanwhile, my brother was busy cleaning the AC filters and measuring the bathroom for safety items—modifying grab bars for a clawfoot tub, bathtub mat, shower stool, toilet elevation kit. He stayed for two weeks, leaving the day before my sister Di arrived.

My relationship with my sister was different. Obviously, with both of them, the conversation was endless, albeit with different subject matter. With Jay, I talked about things like whether it hurt to skydive in the rain. Duh, of course, he'd answer. "Think about it. You're hitting the pointy end of the raindrops." Dad jokes. With Dianne, it was constant arguments about the best way to do things, like where to put your keys when you got home. I favored a small ceramic plate-bowl in the little alcove beside my front door. Dianne gently insisted that it was best to keep them near your purse and wallet wherever they landed. She'd stand beside my bed and we'd hold hands while we argued. Her hands were soft and gentle, like our mother's. At some point, I'd stop her: "You do realize that two women in their seventies talking about their house-key placement is the most boring conversation in the world?" She laughed. For once, we were in perfect agreement.

Dianne's arrival the day after Jay left was fortuitous. As soon as Jay left, I suddenly couldn't walk or lift my arms, leading to privacy issues that only a sister could be trusted to handle. "Don't worry. It's no bother," she'd say. Dianne must have inherited our mother's nursing skills. She knew exactly what to do, handling all the issues that came up with the home care nurse, the PSWs, delivery of the hospital bed and other medical supplies, and arranging extra palliative care. Mike and Lins are lined up to step in (Lindsay joked that he had to fight to get in line to help me). The present system is unsustainable of course. No matter how much my siblings love me, they can't stay forever.

I've been lucky to have had so much time—three years and counting since my initial diagnosis—to process my experience. I've gone through, in no particular order, anger, denial, fear, and moments of acceptance when I'm feeling so sick that ending it all seems more and more appealing. I think about how everyone else's lives will go on. People will remember me—*Oh yeah, Ellen. That was sad. Where do you want to go for lunch?*—but I won't be part of anyone else's narrative anymore.

I've mostly dealt with major regrets, but I admit to occasional sadness at missed opportunities. Little ones, like how I might have made a good TV show given the chance. I still feel a sighing sadness while scrolling through TV menus and finding so much casual, dangerous misogyny. I don't mean the blatantly obvious misogyny of shows that begin with a violently murdered, half-naked, sexy female. I mean the supposedly good shows that should know better. Like *Bosch*. But the first episode I try starts with a photo of a girl who was "raped, murdered and bleached" and ends with a scene featuring a ten-year-old murdered girl on a slab.

I try *House*. The first episode I dip into features cute, thirty-something Dr. Chase treating an extremely pretty nine-year-old girl dying of cancer. She tells him she's never been kissed. She asks him for a kiss. He kisses her on the mouth. Later, he confesses this to the other doctors, and House decides the girl manipulated him because she's oversexualized. Maybe she was molested! Let's further traumatize her by doing a rape kit! I wonder if the show's creator David Shore looks back on that episode now, post #MeToo, and has the common decency to feel utter mortification about its prurient, manipulative, misogynistic portrayal of a prepubescent "femme fatale," and how his show promulgates the trope that men are never responsible for their predatory actions against women and girls. I give *House* another chance and try the next episode, only to see House and Dr. Chase go to the home of their boss, Cuddy, to look for clues about her handyman's strange symptoms after he fell off her roof. House raids Cuddy's underwear drawer and throws a pair of sexy panties at Chase. Then he goes into the bathroom and picks up a box of tampons, commenting archly: "She uses super tampons. What does that mean?" I guess it means she has a large vaginal vault, you creepy piece of shit.

The worst of it is that these seemingly innocuous portrayals of women are shored up by multi-million-dollar budgets, and smart writing and brilliant lighting, and they are molding generations of men and women to think females aren't fully human, that females exist to serve men's needs, that females are ultimately responsible for men's bad decisions. *Eve made him eat the apple. It's her fault.*

At least now, with my double awareness and psilocybin-induced new world view, and loss of lifelong anger, I can move on to happier, or at least more interesting thoughts, like what Heaven might really be like. When I was a child, I hoped it was a place where I'd know what everyone else was thinking. When I told a friend this, she assumed I wanted to know what they were thinking about me. But that wasn't it. I wanted to know what made other people tick. Everyone was such a mystery to me. That's one reason I ended up in journalism, I think. You can interrogate people about almost anything, and, for the most part, they try to give you an honest answer.

Thanks to having cancer, I've had the time and motivation to ponder this, and one conclusion is that maybe it's about feeling lonely; even in the middle of my big family, or among all the friends I'm surrounded by, I can still feel that isolation. How unknowable people are. When I talked to Dr. H. about this, she led me to another possibility—that maybe I was the unknowable one, hiding my true self from other people, and then feeling isolated.

So maybe all my own writing and trying to be honest is about showing myself so that other people might see and understand me.

That is the hope. In the meantime, being able to sit here at my desk and write anything is a gift.

Acknowledgments

The first person I saw when I got back to Toronto in May 2022 was Ian Brown. And the first thing he said to me as we stood in Ramsden Park, me with my doodle and him with his border terrier Harriet, was: *I hope you're taking notes.* I laughed and appreciated the implied compliment. But later, as a lapsed Catholic with neurotic tendencies, I was suspicious. Like, wtf, Brown. Writing is hard. Pitching a book is demeaning. So why would you wish upon me—me! a cancer victim ffs!—the task of excavating my soul for tidbits about the ignominious indignities and excruciating pain of cancer only to then go through the ignominious indignities and excruciating pain of pitching it? Oh well. I must sincerely thank him now for giving me the idea and encouraging me throughout.

I must also thank:

Alyse Frampton, Val Moon, Don Gillmor, and Mary J. de Merindol (an early and helpful reader): friends from across Canada and beyond who have been diligent in checking up on me and helping me keep up my energy and determination to finish this book.

Carl Wilson for his heroic preliminary edit.

Dr. Sarah Hales, the psychiatrist at Princess Margaret, who has saved my life—at least metaphorically—several times during my cancer journey.

Wendy Dennis, for taking me under her wing at Rye High in 1979 and mentoring me through the ins and outs of journalism, life, and loads of laughs.

Denis Pacey for his long-time affection; Ken Finkleman for believing in my talent and encouraging me always.

Art Niemi, a good man who will never forget the affection we shared and still do.

Ken Whyte, my brilliant publisher, editor, and quintessential good sport.

Dr. Anna Spreafico. I love this brilliant, talented, insanely hard-working woman, and I'm so grateful to her and her team for all they did for me—truly above and beyond. Thank you, Anna.

Nora Underwood: Nora has taught me so much about friendship by never letting ours go. I'm forever grateful for her help not only with my big problematic dog, but with life's ongoing challenges—which she has navigated with extraordinary grace.

Morwyn Brebner, a rare and wonderfully weird fellow traveler. She and her family have added so much joy to my life.

Janice Lindsay, David Macfarlane, Ian Pearson, Sue Grimbly, Tecca Crosby, Katie Chisholm, Spencer Robson, Rebecca Young—friends who helped me realize my home now is Toronto, and that good friends will miraculously, happily, instantly offer to take in your big, dirty dog at the drop of an ER-urgent hat.

Johanna Schneller for her baking, her bodaciousness, and her availability in getting me to the hospital whenever urgent care was required.

David Rayner: a man who in another universe would have fit perfectly into my phlegmatic family order if I had the sense to marry him, and in this lifetime, has given me so much comfort and help and knowledge about T-cells and how not to blame them for random events.

Maria Spellman, my grade one BFF, through thick and thin. She prays for me as I sit in abject gratitude for the years of nonsense she has tolerated from me since 1960, for the grace she exhibits to the rest of us while facing bad stuff that bewilderingly happens to the best of good people. I love you, Posyniak.

Cathrin Bradbury: what can I say, except I can't believe my luck in having found this smart, nutty, superstitious, curious, insightful woman to help this prairie girl navigate the ups and downs of Hogtown for the past thirty-odd years.

My family: Eliza, Dianne, Jay, Kaneena, Alec, Miles, Michael, Casey, Jakab, Clare, Leo, Lindsay, Rena, Ruth.

About the Author

Ellen Vanstone was born and raised in Winnipeg, Manitoba, where she attended the University of Winnipeg, majoring in English Literature on a volleyball scholarship. She did a graduate degree in journalism at Ryerson University (now Toronto Metropolitan University) in 1979 and went on to work for a variety of publications, including *The Globe and Mail,* the *National Post, The Walrus,* and *Toronto Life.* She moved into writing for television when her article about working at the newly launched *National Post* won a National Magazine Award for Humour and was optioned by CTV as the basis for a comedy series. That show never made it through the development stage but proved to be the start of a second successful career, which included her co-creation of the award-winning procedural *Rookie Blue.* She died in October 2025.